Just One More Bite!

More Than 150 Mouthwatering Recipes You Just Can't Resist

Best-Selling Author with Millions of Cookbooks Sold

Inquiries should be addressed to:
Cogin, Inc.
1770 NW 64 Street, Suite 500
Fort Lauderdale, FL 33309

MR. FOOD, MR. FOOD TEST KITCHEN, OOH IT'S SO GOOD!!, the Mr. Food likeness and the other MR. FOOD trademarks and logos are trademarks or registered trademarks owned by Ginsburg Enterprises Incorporated and used with permission. All rights reserved.

Library of Congress Cataloging-in-Publication Data
Mr. Food Test Kitchen
     Mr. Food Test Kitchen Just One More Bite!/ Mr. Food

ISBN 978-0-9755396-5-1
1. Cookery. 2. Quick and Easy. I. Title: Mr. Food Test Kitchen Just One More Bite!. II. Title.

Printed in the United States of America

First Edition

www.MrFood.com

Introduction

We've all been there. We put down our fork, and are just about to get up from the table when all of a sudden we say to ourselves, "I think I'll have just one more bite!" It means that the food is so good we just can't leave a single morsel of it behind.

What makes a recipe worthy of being in this book? It's those dishes that are the first to go at the potluck. Or, remember last Thanksgiving when you had to loosen your belt, and even though you felt like you couldn't eat another bite, you asked Uncle Joe to pass the mashed potatoes? That's when you know it's irresistible. And those are the moments we love to help you create at home.

In addition to everyday favorites, this book has many of our most requested holiday recipes that make it practically impossible not to ask for seconds ... or maybe thirds. (We won't count if you don't.) We also share favorite family recipes from our readers, viewers, and even our own Team Members as well as the stories behind the recipes.

Once we collected what we felt was the best of the best recipes (the most irresistible ones), we tested, tasted and retested all of those recipes (while wearing loose fitting pants, of course) and every recipe that ended up with an empty platter was a front runner. So basically, we ate a lot of food and cleaned our plates all throughout this process. (Someone had to do it!) The important thing is that we did all this so you can feel confident about every recipe in this book. They're triple-tested to be so tempting you can't get enough of them.

Besides more than 150 triple-tested recipes and mouthwatering full-color photography throughout the book, you'll find lots of hints and tips from the Mr. Food Test Kitchen to help make cooking a breeze. So go ahead; make just one more recipe. Start the day with our **Maple Walnut Breakfast Buns**, jazz up dinner with the **Rolled Italian Meat Loaf** and wow friends and family with our **Peanut Butter Cream Cheese Pie**. Just don't be surprised if everyone asks for "Just One More Bite." No matter what you choose to make from this book, everyone will be saying, **"OOH IT'S SO GOOD!!®"**

Howard Patty Kelly

Pictured on front cover (l-r): Patty Rosenthal -Test Kitchen Director, Howard Rosenthal - Chief Food Officer, Kelly Rusin - Food Stylist/Photographer.

Acknowledgements

First we want to thank you, our readers and viewers who shared so many of your families' most guarded and cherished recipes. Recipes that are so good that they're worthy of just one more bite.

We couldn't have created all the recipes in this book without our incredibly talented Test Kitchen Director, Patty Rosenthal, who developed as well as ensured that every recipe can be easily recreated at home. We love you Patty! Is that peanut butter pie ready for tasting yet?!

Other members of our Test Kitchen team played an integral role in helping this book come together. Jaime Gross and the rest of the team helped us test, taste and retest every recipe. And while there were rarely any leftovers from the recipes for this book, we still cooked up quite a storm in the kitchen, so we owe a huge thank you to Dave DiCarlo for maintaining the Test Kitchen's showroom-quality shine.

A huge thank you goes to Jodi Flayman for coordinating, documenting and verifying the details on every page. (She was also thorough about trying samples of these recipes.) Many thanks also go to Carol Ginsburg whose proofreading skills ensure that every recipe meets our criteria for being easy to read and accurate. We also have to thank Brenna Fisher for engaging readers with copy to help promote this book—and for keeping us awake with her freshly brewed coffee.

Our company wouldn't be what it is without the behind-the-scenes work of Steve Ginsburg our CEO. Thank you —and thanks for being so good humored when we ate the last bit of banana pudding before you got to it! (Sorry!)

We have to thank Kelly Rusin, our very talented photographer and stylist who once again shared her keen eye and attention to detail when it comes to all of the mouthwatering photos. We also tip our hat to Hal Silverman, for his post-production work that elevated each photo to even loftier drool-worthy status. Also, special thanks go to Lorraine Dan for making these recipes come to life with eye-catching layouts that are beautiful and easy to read.

We also want to thank Alexis Franzi and Jennifer Kramer, our online editors for their contributions and ideas. And we can't forget to thank our office manager, Amy Magro. Without her, we would have a hard time coordinating all the details that go into a book like this.

Finally, *Just One More Bite!* is about loving something so much that you have to go back for more. Here in the Mr. Food Test Kitchen, work is much the same. And no one loves what they do more (or does it better) than Howard Rosenthal. We are so grateful for his creative vision and leadership.

Another person who loved what he did was our founder, Art Ginsburg. Although he is no longer with us, we can't help but feel grateful every day for having known him and having such a wonderful legacy to follow. That will always be "OOH IT'S SO GOOD!! ®"

Contents

Irresistible Breakfasts

Peaches 'n' Cream Dutch Pancake

Serves 6

6 tablespoons (¾ stick) butter, melted

6 eggs

1 cup milk

½ teaspoon salt

1 cup all-purpose flour

2 tablespoons (¼ stick) butter

½ cup light brown sugar

6 peaches, thinly sliced

Frozen whipped topping, thawed, for garnish

Confectioners' sugar for sprinkling

1 Preheat oven to 425 degrees F. Pour the melted butter into a 9- x 13-inch baking dish; set aside.

2 In a blender, combine eggs, milk, and salt; blend until frothy. Slowly add flour, mixing until well blended. Pour egg mixture into baking dish.

3 Bake 25 to 30 minutes, or until golden brown and center is set.

4 Meanwhile, in a skillet over medium heat, melt 2 tablespoons butter. Add brown sugar and peaches. Sauté 1 to 2 minutes, or until softened. Spoon peaches over pancake, top with whipped topping, and sprinkle with confectioners' sugar. Serve immediately.

About This Recipe:

When we took this out of the oven and topped it with the peaches, the whipped topping, and the confectioners' sugar, we had a hunch that this recipe was right for this book. But after our whole team tried it, there was no question that this is absolutely one of those dishes that had everyone saying... "Can I have just one more bite?"

Silver Dollar Chocolate Chip Pancakes

Serves 8

- 2 cups pancake and baking mix
- 1 cup club soda
- 2 eggs
- 1 teaspoon vanilla extract
- 1 teaspoon sugar
- 1 cup (6 ounces) semisweet mini chocolate chips
- 2 tablespoons vegetable shortening, divided

1 In a large bowl, combine baking mix, club soda, eggs, vanilla, and sugar; mix well. Stir in chocolate chips until well combined.

2 On a nonstick griddle or in a large skillet over medium heat, melt 1 tablespoon vegetable shortening. Pour 1 tablespoon batter per pancake onto griddle and cook pancakes about 2 minutes, or until bubbles appear on top. Flip pancakes and cook 1 to 2 more minutes, or until golden on both sides, adding more shortening as needed. Serve immediately, or keep warm in a low oven until all pancakes are cooked.

Test Kitchen Hints & Tips — Mr. Food

The secret to these is the club soda...its bubbles add air to the batter making them some of the lightest and fluffiest pancakes ever. They may be small in size but they are huge when it comes to the "yum" factor.

Mini Sausage and Cheese Quiches

Makes 12

12 round butter-flavored crackers

2 eggs, beaten

1 cup (½ pint) heavy cream

2 cups (8 ounces) shredded
Cheddar cheese

⅓ cup cooked sausage crumbles

1 Preheat oven to 400 degrees F. Coat a 12-cup muffin tin with cooking spray. Place one cracker in bottom of each muffin cup.

2 In a medium bowl, combine remaining ingredients; mix well then spoon mixture equally into muffin cups.

3 Bake 18 to 20 minutes, or until golden. Serve immediately.

We Dare You!

Are you up for a challenge? If so, just try eating one of these and walking away from the table. We bet there will be a little voice in your head calling you back for another and another...

Sausage Pinwheels

Makes 16

1 (16-ounce) package spicy pork sausage (such as Jimmy Dean)

½ red bell pepper, diced

4 scallions, thinly sliced

2 (8-ounce) packages refrigerated crescent rolls (8 rolls each)

1 Preheat oven to 400 degrees F.

2 In a bowl, combine sausage, red pepper, and scallions; mix well. Unroll one package of crescent rolls and press seams together to form one large rectangle. Repeat with second package of crescent rolls.

3 Spread half of sausage mixture evenly over each rectangle; starting from narrow end, roll up jelly-roll style. Cut each roll into eight equal slices and place each on its side on a baking sheet.

4 Bake 25 to 30 minutes, or until sausage is no longer pink and crust is golden. Serve warm.

Test Kitchen, Mr. Food Hints & Tips

Although this recipe makes 16 pinwheels, let us assure you that it doesn't feed 16 people. It's an old southern favorite that is so good you can't stop at two, never mind just one. Just in case there are any left, a little tip – they do reheat well in the toaster oven.

Extra Special Eggs Benedict

Serves 4

1 (1.25-ounce) package hollandaise sauce mix, prepared according to package directions

6 cups water

½ cup white vinegar

8 eggs

4 English muffins, split and toasted

4 ounces sliced smoked salmon (lox), divided

1 Warm the hollandaise sauce over low heat.

2 Meanwhile, in a large skillet, bring water and vinegar to a boil. Crack eggs one at a time and gently drop each into boiling water mixture. Cook 4 to 6 minutes, or until eggs are firm on the outside.

3 Place toasted English muffin halves on a platter and top each evenly with smoked salmon. Then, using a slotted spoon, place an egg over each. Top eggs with hollandaise sauce and serve immediately.

Serving Suggestion:
If you want to make this more traditional, just substitute Canadian bacon slices or sausage patties for the smoked salmon.

Tempting Breads & Muffins

Lemon Raspberry Swirl Bread

Makes 1 loaf

1 (11-ounce) package refrigerated French loaf bread

¼ cup raspberry jam

¼ cup dried cranberries

½ cup confectioners' sugar

1-½ teaspoons lemon juice

1 Preheat oven to 350 degrees F. Coat a rimmed baking sheet with cooking spray.

2 Unroll bread dough into rectangle. Spread jam over dough and sprinkle with dried cranberries. Roll up dough, starting at short side. Place seam side down on prepared baking sheet.

3 Bake 25 to 30 minutes, or until golden. Let cool on a wire rack at least 1 hour.

4 In a medium bowl, combine confectioners' sugar and lemon juice, stirring until smooth; drizzle over loaf. Slice and serve.

We Dare You!

Are you a sucker when it comes to fresh-out–of-the-oven bread? If so, we have to warn you... this is not easy to resist. Between the sweet aroma of it drifting through your house and the tart lemon glaze dripping off of it, there is little chance that you won't be digging in even before it cools.

Easy Friendship Bread

Makes 2 loaves

2-¾ cups all-purpose flour

1-¾ cups sugar

2 teaspoons cinnamon

1-½ teaspoons baking powder

½ teaspoon baking soda

½ teaspoon salt

1 (4-serving-size) package instant vanilla pudding mix

1-¼ cups milk

1 cup vegetable oil

3 eggs

1 teaspoon vanilla extract

1 Preheat oven to 325 degrees F. Coat two 9- x 5-inch loaf pans with cooking spray.

2 In a large bowl, mix flour, sugar, cinnamon, baking powder, baking soda, salt, and pudding mix; set aside.

3 In a medium bowl, whisk milk, oil, eggs, and vanilla. Stir liquid mixture into flour mixture and combine well. Evenly divide mixture into prepared pans.

4 Bake 55 to 60 minutes, or until a toothpick inserted in center comes out clean. Let cool 15 minutes, then invert on wire rack and finish cooling.

Did You Know?

This recipe is based on the traditional Amish friendship bread that has been around for decades. It's one of those recipes, hence it's name, that's made to be shared. That's why we made sure the recipe makes two loaves, one for you and one to pass on to a good friend.

Parmesan Onion Board

Serves 12

2 tablespoons butter

1 onion, very thinly sliced

1 pound frozen bread dough, thawed

1 egg, beaten

½ teaspoon poppy seeds

½ cup shredded Parmesan cheese

1 Preheat oven to 350 degrees F. Coat a large rimmed baking sheet with cooking spray.

2 In a medium skillet over medium heat, melt butter and cook onion 6 to 8 minutes, or until soft and lightly browned.

3 On a lightly floured surface, roll out dough to a 10- x 15-inch rectangle. With your fingertips, gently spread dough to cover pan, and push it up to the edges, forming a rim. If dough is too sticky, dust it and your hands lightly with flour.

4 Brush dough with beaten egg, then spread cooked onion evenly over the top. Sprinkle with poppy seeds and Parmesan cheese, and bake 25 to 30 minutes, or until golden.

5 Remove to a cutting board; let cool slightly, then cut into squares and serve.

Mini Double Chocolate Muffins

Makes 36 mini muffins

1-½ cups all-purpose flour

1 tablespoon baking powder

¼ teaspoon salt

½ cup sugar

½ cup unsweetened cocoa

2 eggs, beaten

¾ cup milk

1 stick butter, melted

⅓ cup mini semisweet chocolate chips

1 Preheat oven to 350 degrees F. Place paper liners in 3 (12-cup) mini muffin tins.

2 In a large bowl, combine flour, baking powder, salt, sugar, and cocoa. Add eggs, milk, and butter; mix well with a spoon. Add chocolate chips and mix just until combined. (Batter will be stiff.) Fill each muffin cup with batter, distributing evenly.

3 Bake 15 to 18 minutes, or until a toothpick inserted in center comes out clean. Remove muffins from pan and cool on a wire rack.

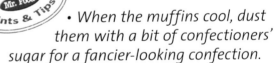

Test Kitchen. Mr. Food Hints & Tips

- *When the muffins cool, dust them with a bit of confectioners' sugar for a fancier-looking confection.*

- *If you don't have mini paper liners, you can coat the pans with cooking spray instead.*

- *You can also bake these in a 12-cup muffin tin for regular-sized muffins. Just adjust your baking time accordingly.*

Parmesan Onion Board

Serves 12

2 tablespoons butter

1 onion, very thinly sliced

1 pound frozen bread dough, thawed

1 egg, beaten

½ teaspoon poppy seeds

½ cup shredded Parmesan cheese

1 Preheat oven to 350 degrees F. Coat a large rimmed baking sheet with cooking spray.

2 In a medium skillet over medium heat, melt butter and cook onion 6 to 8 minutes, or until soft and lightly browned.

3 On a lightly floured surface, roll out dough to a 10- x 15-inch rectangle. With your fingertips, gently spread dough to cover pan, and push it up to the edges, forming a rim. If dough is too sticky, dust it and your hands lightly with flour.

4 Brush dough with beaten egg, then spread cooked onion evenly over the top. Sprinkle with poppy seeds and Parmesan cheese, and bake 25 to 30 minutes, or until golden.

5 Remove to a cutting board; let cool slightly, then cut into squares and serve.

Mini Double Chocolate Muffins

Makes 36 mini muffins

1-½ cups all-purpose flour

1 tablespoon baking powder

¼ teaspoon salt

½ cup sugar

½ cup unsweetened cocoa

2 eggs, beaten

¾ cup milk

1 stick butter, melted

⅓ cup mini semisweet chocolate chips

1 Preheat oven to 350 degrees F. Place paper liners in 3 (12-cup) mini muffin tins.

2 In a large bowl, combine flour, baking powder, salt, sugar, and cocoa. Add eggs, milk, and butter; mix well with a spoon. Add chocolate chips and mix just until combined. (Batter will be stiff.) Fill each muffin cup with batter, distributing evenly.

3 Bake 15 to 18 minutes, or until a toothpick inserted in center comes out clean. Remove muffins from pan and cool on a wire rack.

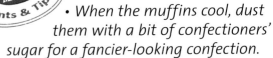

• When the muffins cool, dust them with a bit of confectioners' sugar for a fancier-looking confection.

• If you don't have mini paper liners, you can coat the pans with cooking spray instead.

• You can also bake these in a 12-cup muffin tin for regular-sized muffins. Just adjust your baking time accordingly.

Amazing Appetizers

Cheesy Italian Stuffed Meatballs

Makes 20

½ pound ground pork

½ pound ground beef

½ cup Italian bread crumbs

½ cup grated Parmesan cheese

½ cup water

1 teaspoon Italian seasoning

1 egg

1-½ teaspoons garlic powder

1 teaspoon salt

¾ teaspoon black pepper

1 (8-ounce) package mozzarella cheese, cut into 20 (½-inch) cubes

1 Preheat oven to 350 degrees F. Coat a baking sheet with cooking spray.

2 In a large bowl, combine all ingredients except mozzarella cheese; mix well.

3 Divide mixture into 20 meatballs, then form each meatball around a mozzarella cube, making sure to cover cheese completely. Place on prepared baking sheet.

4 Bake 15 to 20 minutes, or until no longer pink in center. Serve immediately.

Test Kitchen Mr. Food Hints & Tips

Make sure the mozzarella cheese is cold when you insert it into the meatball as this will minimize it from oozing out during baking. Oh, and don't forget to serve up a bowl of spaghetti sauce with this for dunkin'.

5-Minute Bruschetta

Serves 8

1 loaf French bread, sliced into
  1-inch-thick slices

Cooking spray

⅓ cup olive oil

1 tablespoon balsamic vinegar

⅓ cup chopped fresh basil

1 teaspoon salt

1 teaspoon black pepper

10 plum tomatoes, seeded and
  chopped

1 Preheat broiler. Coat a baking sheet with cooking spray. Place bread slices on baking sheet and lightly spray tops with cooking spray.

2 Broil 2 to 3 minutes, or until golden. Place on a serving platter.

3 In a large bowl, combine remaining ingredients; mix until well blended, then spoon over toasted bread. Serve immediately.

Note:

To seed the plum tomatoes, cut them in half lengthwise and gently squeeze to release the seeds.

"When my wife and I moved into our new house, one of the first things we did was to plant a small vegetable garden. Well, within months we had more tomatoes than we knew what to do with. So we came up with this quick bruschetta as a way to use them up. These were almost addictive."

Tom M., Bouckville, NY

Fried Mac 'n' Cheese Balls

Makes 22

1 (12-ounce) package frozen macaroni & cheese, thawed

1 egg

1 tablespoon water

1 cup Italian bread crumbs

½ teaspoon garlic powder

½ teaspoon black pepper

1-½ cups vegetable oil

1 Using a small ice cream scoop or a teaspoon, shape macaroni and cheese into 1-inch balls and place on a wax paper-lined baking sheet. Freeze 2 hours, or until frozen firm.

2 In a shallow dish, beat egg and water. In another shallow dish, combine bread crumbs, garlic powder, and black pepper.

3 In a deep saucepan over medium heat, heat oil until hot.

4 Dip frozen balls into egg wash then roll in bread crumbs. In small batches, fry balls 3 to 5 minutes, or until golden brown and center is hot. (Keep remaining balls frozen until ready to fry.) Drain on a paper towel-lined plate and serve immediately.

Test Kitchen. Mr. Food Hints & Tips

There is no need to heat the macaroni and cheese before rolling into balls, just thaw it. If you have left over homemade mac 'n' cheese, you can use that instead of the frozen. Just make sure it's chilled before rolling into balls.

Simple Stuffed Mushrooms

Makes 12 to 15

1 pound large fresh mushrooms

3 tablespoons butter

¼ cup seasoned bread crumbs

¼ teaspoon onion powder

¼ teaspoon garlic powder

¼ teaspoon salt

⅛ teaspoon black pepper

2 tablespoons sour cream

1 Preheat oven to 350 degrees F.

2 Gently clean mushrooms by wiping with a damp cloth. Remove stems from ¾ of the mushrooms; set aside those caps. Finely chop stems and remaining mushrooms.

3 In a large skillet over medium heat, melt butter; sauté chopped mushrooms 4 to 5 minutes, or until softened. Remove from heat and add remaining ingredients; mix well.

4 Using a teaspoon, stuff mushroom caps with stuffing mixture. Place on an ungreased rimmed baking sheet.

5 Bake 15 to 20 minutes, or until warmed through. Serve immediately.

Serving Suggestion:
These are so simple and are the perfect finger food. We've also served these topped with some hollandaise sauce for an incredible go-along with grilled steak.

Raspberry Bacon Shrimp
Makes 40

40 large shrimp, peeled and deveined, with tails on, (about 1-½ pounds)

20 bacon slices

½ cup seedless raspberry jam

¼ cup sweet chili sauce

1 Preheat oven to broil. Coat 2 baking sheets with cooking spray.

2 Cut bacon slices in half crosswise. Wrap bacon pieces around shrimp, placing seam side down on prepared baking sheets.

3 In a small bowl, mix raspberry jam and sweet chili sauce. Reserve ¼ cup of sauce. Brush shrimp and bacon with remaining sauce.

4 Broil shrimp about 3 inches from heat 4 to 5 minutes, or until bacon is crisp and shrimp is pink. (Make sure you keep oven door open slightly.) Serve with remaining sauce.

Did You Know?
When you buy shrimp you will see a number on the bag or in the seafood case. That number tells you how many of that size shrimp are in a pound. The smaller the number, the bigger the shrimp. We like using 25-30 per pound for these.

Dressed Up Weenie Wellingtons

Makes 24

1 stick butter, melted

½ cup chopped walnuts

3 tablespoons honey

3 tablespoons brown sugar

1 (8-ounce) package refrigerated crescent rolls

24 mini hot dogs or mini sausages

1 Preheat oven to 400 degrees F.

2 In a 9- x 13-inch baking dish, combine butter, walnuts, honey, and brown sugar.

3 Unroll dough and separate into 8 triangles. Cut each triangle into 3 smaller triangles. Place a hot dog on the wide end of each triangle. Roll up and place seam side down on top of butter mixture. Repeat with all hot dogs.

4 Bake 15 to 20 minutes, or until dough is golden brown. Allow to cool 3 to 5 minutes and serve.

"I started making this recipe years ago and now whenever I go to a party this is always what I'm asked to bring. They must be good as they're always the first thing gone from the table!"

Amy M., Mr. Food Test Kitchen Office Manager

Garlic Lovers' Chicken Wings

Serves 4

2 bulbs fresh garlic, separated into cloves and peeled

1 cup olive oil

1 teaspoon salt

1 cup grated Parmesan cheese

⅛ teaspoon cayenne pepper

1 cup seasoned bread crumbs

½ teaspoon black pepper

4 pounds frozen chicken wings, thawed, dried well

1 Preheat oven to 375 degrees F. Coat 2 rimmed baking sheets with cooking spray.

2 In a blender or food processor, puree garlic, olive oil, and salt. Pour into a bowl.

3 In a separate bowl, mix together the Parmesan cheese, cayenne pepper, bread crumbs, and black pepper.

4 Dip the wings, one at a time, in the garlic puree then roll them in the bread crumb mixture, coating them completely. Place on prepared baking sheets in a single layer.

5 Bake 55 to 60 minutes, or until no pink remains and wings are golden brown.

About This Recipe:

We've tested and tasted lots of wing recipes over the years and these Garlic Lovers' Chicken Wings are second to none. Every time we would eat one, we all said, "Ok, this is the last one," but just minutes later we all found ourselves going back for more.

Mexican Potluck

Serves 18

1 (10-½-ounce) package ranch-flavored tortilla chips, finely crushed

½ stick butter, melted

2 (16-ounce) cans refried beans

1 (1-¼ ounce) package taco seasoning mix

1-½ cups shredded cooked chicken

1 cup prepared guacamole

1 (8-ounce) container sour cream

2 (2-¼-ounce) cans sliced ripe olives

1 tomato, seeded and chopped

1 (8-ounce) package pepper jack cheese, shredded

Tortilla chips for serving

1 Preheat oven to 350 degrees F. Lightly coat a 9- or 10-inch springform pan with cooking spray.

2 Combine crushed tortilla chips and butter; press into bottom and 1 inch up sides of prepared pan. Bake 10 minutes. Cool on a wire rack.

3 In a medium bowl, combine refried beans and taco seasoning mix, stirring well; spread over prepared crust. Sprinkle shredded chicken over beans, then layer guacamole, sour cream, olives, tomatoes, and cheese over chicken. Cover and chill 1 hour.

4 Place on a serving plate, and remove sides of springform pan. Serve with tortilla chips.

Test Kitchen. Mr. Food Hints & Tips — *The easiest way to crush the tortilla chips? Just place them in a resealable plastic bag, seal the bag, and have at it with a rolling pin or a can of veggies.*

Rancher's Buttermilk Chicken Bites

Serves 8

¾ cup buttermilk

1 egg

1 cup self-rising flour

1 tablespoon confectioners' sugar

1 teaspoon paprika

2 teaspoons salt

½ teaspoon black pepper

1-½ pounds boneless, skinless chicken breasts, cut into 1-inch pieces

1 cup vegetable oil

1 cup barbecue sauce

½ cup honey

1 tablespoon yellow mustard

1 In a small bowl, combine buttermilk and egg; beat well. In a medium bowl, combine flour, sugar, paprika, salt, and pepper; mix well.

2 Dip chicken in flour mixture then in buttermilk mixture, then in flour mixture again, coating completely.

3 In a large skillet over medium heat, heat oil until hot but not smoking. Add chicken in batches and cook 4 to 5 minutes, or until no pink remains and coating is golden, stirring occasionally.

4 Meanwhile, in a medium bowl, combine barbecue sauce, honey and mustard.

5 Remove chicken to a paper towel-lined platter to drain. Serve immediately with dipping sauce.

About This Recipe:
This dish was inspired by a trip we took to Dallas a few years ago to tape a show. The basket of chicken bites that we were served was just as memorable as the honey mustard barbecue sauce that they served with it.

Really Loaded Nacho Fries

Serves 6

- 1 (22-ounce) package frozen waffle fries
- 1 pound ground beef
- 1 (1-¼-ounce) package taco seasoning mix
- 1 (16-ounce) can refried beans
- 2 cups (8 ounces) shredded Mexican cheese blend
- 1 (2-¼-ounce) can sliced black olives, drained
- 1 (4-ounce) can chopped green chilies, drained
- ¾ cup salsa
- ½ cup sour cream
- 1 scallion, thinly sliced
- 2 tablespoons chopped fresh cilantro

1 Preheat oven to 400 degrees F. Coat a baking sheet with cooking spray. Place waffle fries in a single layer on baking sheet. Bake 20 to 25 minutes, or until crispy.

2 Meanwhile, in a large skillet over medium-high heat, brown ground beef 7 to 10 minutes, or until no pink remains, stirring occasionally to crumble. Stir in taco seasoning and refried beans. Cook 3 to 5 additional minutes, or until thoroughly heated.

3 Spoon mixture over fries, then top with shredded cheese, olives, and chilies.

4 Return to oven 4 to 5 minutes, or until cheese is melted. Remove from oven and top with salsa, sour cream, scallion, and cilantro. Serve immediately.

Serving Suggestion:

If you want to serve these during a football-watching party, you can keep these warm by placing the baking sheet on top of an electric griddle set on very low. Just make sure you let everyone know the tray will be hot, but so will your fries.

Bread Bowl Spinach Dip

Serves 16

1 (10-ounce) package frozen chopped spinach, thawed, drained

1 (16-ounce) container sour cream

1 cup mayonnaise

1 (1.4-ounce) package vegetable soup mix

2 garlic cloves, minced

1 (14-ounce) can artichoke hearts, drained and coarsely chopped

1 (1-pound) round loaf of bread

1 In a medium bowl, combine all ingredients except bread; mix well. Refrigerate 2 hours, or until ready to serve.

2 When ready to serve, using a serrated knife, cut a hole in top of bread about 3 inches in diameter. Hollow out bread, leaving 1 inch of bread around sides. Stir dip then spoon into bread bowl. Cut bread top and hollowed-out pieces into 1-inch chunks for dipping.

Serving Suggestion:
Since this makes a lot, you may want to pick up an extra bread to cut up for dipping as well as some cut-up veggies. This way you get to enjoy every last spoonful.

BLT Spread

Serves 10

- 1 (8-ounce) package cream cheese, softened
- ½ cup mayonnaise
- ¼ teaspoon salt
- ¼ teaspoon black pepper
- 2 cups chopped iceberg lettuce
- 1 (4.5-ounce) package real bacon pieces
- 4 plum tomatoes, chopped
- 2 scallions, chopped
- 1 cup shredded sharp Cheddar cheese

1 In a medium bowl, combine cream cheese, mayonnaise, salt, and pepper; mix well.

2 Mound on a serving platter, top evenly with remaining ingredients, and chill until ready to serve.

Did You Know?

This recipe is an old favorite of the Mr. Food Test Kitchen. Although we have featured this a number of times, we thought it wouldn't be fair if we left it out of this book since it's definitely one of those recipes that once you start eating, you find yourself saying... "Oh, just one more bite".

Baked Tomato Pesto Dip

Serves 16

- 2 (8-ounce) packages cream cheese, softened
- ½ cup plus 1 tablespoon grated Parmesan cheese, divided
- ⅓ cup mayonnaise
- 2 tablespoons fresh lemon juice
- 1 teaspoon garlic powder
- ½ teaspoon onion powder
- 10 sun-dried tomatoes (about ½ cup)
- ½ cup walnuts, toasted
- ⅓ cup packed fresh basil leaves

1 Preheat oven to 350 degrees F. Coat a 9-inch pie plate with cooking spray.

2 In a medium bowl, beat cream cheese, ½ cup Parmesan cheese, the mayonnaise, lemon juice, garlic powder, and onion powder until well blended.

3 In a blender or food processor, combine sun-dried tomatoes, walnuts, and basil; process until finely chopped.

4 Add tomato mixture to cream cheese mixture; mix well then spoon into prepared pie plate. Sprinkle with remaining Parmesan cheese.

5 Bake 25 to 30 minutes, or until heated through. Serve immediately.

Lighten It Up!

If you love a dip that's creamy and packed with flavor, there's no need to flip any more pages until you make this. Now, if you're also looking to cut back here and there, we've made this with low-fat cream cheese and mayo and the results were still quite tasty.

Sweet & Crunchy Stuffed Brie

Serves 10

1 (8-ounce) package refrigerated crescent rolls

1 (8-ounce) Brie cheese round, well chilled

⅓ cup apricot pineapple preserves

¼ cup chopped pecans

1 egg, beaten

1 Preheat oven to 350 degrees F. Unroll dough and pinch seams together.

2 Slice Brie in half horizontally and place bottom half in center of dough. Spread preserves over cut side, sprinkle with pecans, and replace top of Brie. Bring dough up over top of Brie, pressing firmly to seal. Place seam side down on baking sheet and brush with beaten egg.

3 Bake 25 to 30 minutes, or until golden. Let cool 5 to 10 minutes before serving.

Did You Know?

The white outer part of Brie, known as the rind, is edible. Although some folks carve around it, it's perfectly safe to eat and in France if you don't eat it they may look at you strangely. Just keep that in mind when you are in Paris.

Mouthwatering Main Dishes

Chicken Divan Casserole

Serves 6

2 (10-¾-ounce) cans cream of broccoli soup

1 cup mayonnaise

¾ cup milk

½ teaspoon garlic powder

½ teaspoon salt

¼ teaspoon black pepper

1 (16-ounce) package frozen chopped broccoli, thawed and drained

2-½ cups diced cooked chicken

1-½ cups (6 ounces) shredded Cheddar cheese

¾ cup coarsely crushed butter-flavored crackers

2 tablespoons (¼ stick) butter, melted

1 Preheat oven to 350 degrees F. Coat a 2-quart baking dish with cooking spray.

2 In a large bowl, combine soup, mayonnaise, milk, garlic powder, salt, and pepper; mix well. Stir in broccoli, chicken, and cheese. Pour into prepared baking dish.

3 In a small bowl, mix crackers and butter and sprinkle on top of casserole.

4 Bake uncovered 35 to 40 minutes, or until hot.

About This Recipe:

Casseroles like this are some of the easiest and most popular go-to weeknight options there are. They're one-pot wonders that deliver every time and as for the taste, you can let us know after you're done with your second helping!

Yiayia's Chicken

Serves 6

¼ cup olive oil

6 chicken thighs with skin

1 yellow onion, diced

1 (6-ounce) can tomato paste

6 cups water

2 cinnamon sticks

6 whole cloves

1 tablespoon salt

1 pound spaghetti

¼ cup grated Romano cheese

1 In a soup pot over medium heat, heat oil just until smoking.

2 Sauté chicken thighs, skin side down, 5 minutes. Turn over and sauté 5 more minutes. Remove chicken from pot and set aside.

3 Add onions to the pot and sauté about 5 minutes, or until translucent. Return chicken to the pot, along with tomato paste, water, cinnamon sticks, cloves, and salt; stir to blend completely. Turn heat to medium-low, cover, and cook 1-½ hours, stirring occasionally.

4 Meanwhile, cook spaghetti according to package directions. Drain and serve with chicken and sauce. Sprinkle with Romano cheese.

"My Greek Yiayia (grandmother) & Mama served this to us as kids. Now that I'm a mom, it's become a weekly tradition in our house. It's a hearty and economical dinner that brings back memories of my Yiayia every time I serve it."

Patty M., Lighthouse Point, FL

Engagement Chicken

Serves 4 (but should be served only for 2)

2 tablespoons vegetable oil

1 teaspoon paprika

½ teaspoon onion powder

½ teaspoon garlic powder

½ teaspoon salt

½ teaspoon black pepper

1 (4- to 4-½-pound) chicken

4 sprigs fresh rosemary, plus more for garnish

2 lemons, cut in half

½ cup white wine

1 Preheat oven to 350 degrees F.

2 In a small bowl, combine oil, paprika, onion powder, garlic powder, salt, and pepper. Place chicken in a roasting pan and rub seasoning mixture over chicken until completely coated. Stuff rosemary sprigs and 2 lemon halves inside cavity. Squeeze remaining 2 lemon halves over chicken and then place in pan. Pour white wine over chicken.

3 Bake uncovered 1-½ hours or until chicken skin is crispy and juices run clear, basting occasionally with pan juices. Remove from oven and discard rosemary and lemon halves.

4 Place chicken on a serving platter garnished with extra rosemary sprigs and serve.

Did You Know?

The story behind this recipe is that it's so good, that when a girl makes this for her boyfriend, he'll like it so much he'll ask her to marry him. Now we don't make any guarantees about the engagement part, but we can tell ya that he'll be thinking, "With cooking like this, what's not to love?" Sorry, the ring is not included!

Cowboy Chicken Casserole

Serves 6

1 (10-¾-ounce) can cream of chicken soup

1 (14.5-ounce) can diced tomatoes

1 cup frozen corn, thawed

1 (2.25-ounce) can sliced black olives, drained

2 teaspoons chili powder

2 teaspoons cumin

½ teaspoon salt

12 corn tortillas, cut into ½-inch strips

4 cups shredded cooked chicken

1 cup sliced scallions

2 cups (8 ounces) shredded Mexican cheese blend

1 Preheat oven to 350 degrees F. Coat a 9- x 13-inch baking dish with cooking spray.

2 In a bowl, combine soup, tomatoes, corn, black olives, chili powder, cumin, and salt.

3 Line bottom of prepared baking dish with half the tortilla strips. Sprinkle half the chicken over the tortilla strips. Top with half the soup mixture, half the scallions, and half the cheese. Repeat layers.

4 Bake 30 to 35 minutes, or until bubbly and hot.

"This casserole has been in our family for years. When we were young, my Mom told my brothers and me that if we ate this, we would grow up and be big and strong like the cowboys we loved watching on TV. We didn't turn into cowboys, but we still serve this when the whole family gets together."
Doug H., Scottsdale, AZ

Cheesy Cornbread & Chili Bake

Serves 8

2 tablespoons vegetable oil

1 large onion, chopped

3 garlic cloves, minced

2 pounds ground beef

1 (28-ounce) can crushed tomatoes

2 tablespoons chili powder

1 teaspoon ground cumin

1 teaspoon salt

1 teaspoon black pepper

2 (16-ounce) cans red kidney beans, drained

1 (8.5-ounce) package corn muffin mix

1 cup (4 ounces) shredded Mexican cheese blend

1 In a large pot, heat oil over medium-high heat; sauté onion and garlic 5 minutes, or until tender. Add ground beef and brown 8 to 10 minutes, or until no pink remains; drain off excess liquid. Add remaining ingredients except muffin mix and cheese; mix well. Cover and simmer over low heat 20 to 25 minutes, or until thickened.

2 Preheat oven to 375 degrees F. Coat a 9- x 13-inch baking dish with cooking spray.

3 Spoon chili into prepared baking dish. Prepare muffin mix as directed on package; stir in cheese. Spread over chili.

4 Bake 20 minutes, or until a toothpick inserted in center comes out clean. Cool slightly and serve.

Over the Top:

To take this over the top, right before serving, brush some melted butter over the cornbread to make it extra delicious.

Rolled Italian Meat Loaf

Serves 6

2 pounds lean ground beef

3 slices white bread, torn into small pieces

2 eggs

1-¼ cups spaghetti sauce, divided

1 teaspoon Italian seasoning

1 teaspoon garlic powder

1 teaspoon salt

¼ teaspoon black pepper

2 cups (8 ounces) shredded mozzarella cheese

¼ cup fresh basil, slivered

1. Preheat oven to 350 degrees F. Coat a 9- x 13-inch baking dish with cooking spray.

2. In a large bowl, combine ground beef, bread, eggs, ¼ cup spaghetti sauce, Italian seasoning, garlic powder, salt, and pepper. Mix with your hands until well blended. Place on a 12- x 16-inch piece of wax paper and pat firmly into a 10- x 12-inch rectangle.

3. Sprinkle cheese and basil evenly over ground beef. Roll up jelly roll-style, starting from the short end, by lifting the wax paper and removing it as you roll. Seal ends well. Place seam side down in prepared baking dish. Pour ½ cup spaghetti sauce over top.

4. Bake 45 minutes. Remove from oven, pour remaining sauce over meat, and return to oven 10 to 15 minutes, or until no pink remains. Remove from oven and allow to stand 5 minutes. Slice and serve.

"My family doesn't usually like meat loaf, but when I made it like this, they LOVED it! I guess the mixture of the flavors, the cheesiness, and the coating of spaghetti sauce, have made this our new go-to dinner.

Jodi F., Mr. Food Test Kitchen Project Coordinator

Weeknight Beef Stroganoff

Serves 4

½ pound egg noodles

4 tablespoons (½ stick) butter

1-½ pounds boneless beef top sirloin steak, cut into ¼-inch strips

¼ cup finely chopped onion

1 garlic clove, minced

2 tablespoons all-purpose flour

½ teaspoon black pepper

1 (10-¾-ounce) can cream of mushroom soup

1 (10-¾-ounce) can cream of chicken soup

¼ pound fresh mushrooms, sliced

1 cup sour cream

1. Cook egg noodles according to package directions. Drain and keep warm.

2. Meanwhile, in a large skillet over medium heat, melt butter. Add steak, onion, and garlic, and cook 5 to 7 minutes, or until steak is no longer pink, stirring frequently.

3. Add flour and pepper; mix well. Add the soups and mushrooms; mix well. Reduce heat to low and simmer 8 to 10 minutes, or until beef is tender.

4. Just before serving, stir in sour cream and cook 2 to 4 minutes, or until mixture is heated through. Serve immediately over cooked noodles.

Fresh Salmon Burgers with Dill Sauce

Serves 4

1 (1.25-ounce) envelope Hollandaise sauce mix

¼ cup mayonnaise

¼ cup sour cream

1 teaspoon dried dillweed

1 teaspoon Worcestershire sauce

⅛ teaspoon plus ¼ teaspoon salt, divided

1 pound skinless salmon fillets, cut into chunks

1 to 2 slices fresh white bread, torn up

2 scallions, sliced

1 tablespoon lemon juice

¼ teaspoon black pepper

1 In a saucepan, prepare Hollandaise sauce according to package directions. Mix in mayonnaise, sour cream, dillweed, Worcestershire sauce, and ⅛ teaspoon salt. Pour into a bowl and refrigerate until ready to serve.

2 In a food processor, place salmon, bread, scallions, lemon juice, remaining salt, and the pepper; pulse until coarsely chopped and well combined. Form mixture into 4 burgers.

3 Coat a skillet or grill pan with cooking spray. Over medium-high heat, cook burgers 3 to 4 minutes per side, or until cooked through. Serve with sauce.

Did You Know?
Fresh salmon is packed with beneficial Omega-3 fatty acids, is heart healthy, and besides all that, it really tastes great.

Georgia Peach Glazed Ham

Serves 10

1 (5- to 6-pound) fully cooked semi-boneless cured ham

½ cup honey

1 cup peach preserves

⅛ teaspoon ground cinnamon

1 Preheat oven to 325 degrees F. Using a sharp knife, score the ham about ¼ inch deep in a crisscross pattern. Place ham in a large roasting pan.

2 Meanwhile, in a small saucepan, combine remaining ingredients; mix well and heat until warm.

3 Pour half the glaze over ham and roast 30 minutes. Baste with remaining glaze, and continue to cook an additional 45 minutes, or until heated through. Let ham sit 10 minutes before slicing.

Test Kitchen. Mr. Food. Hints & Tips *The reason we suggest that you score the ham is that it prevents the glaze from sliding off the ham. It also helps the flavors penetrate, giving it more flavor through and through.*

Texas BBQ Mac & Cheese

Serves 6

3 tablespoons butter

2 tablespoons all-purpose flour

2 cups milk

½ teaspoon salt

¼ teaspoon black pepper

2 cups (8 ounces) shredded sharp Cheddar cheese

1 (8-ounce) package elbow macaroni, cooked and drained

1 (16-ounce) container refrigerated barbecue pulled pork

1 cup coarsely crumbled corn chips

1 Preheat oven to 350 degrees F. Coat a 2-quart casserole dish with cooking spray.

2 In a large saucepan over low heat, melt butter. Stir in flour, and cook 1 to 2 minutes. Add milk, salt, and pepper, and cook over medium heat until mixture starts to bubble, stirring occasionally. Remove mixture from heat and add cheese, stirring until melted. Add macaroni; mix well then pour into prepared baking dish.

3 Spread pulled pork over macaroni and cheese and top with crushed corn chips.

4 Bake 20 to 25 minutes, or until heated through.

"Living outside of Dallas all our life, my husband and I grew up on barbecue. With both of us working, we're always looking for new dinner ideas for us and our 3 girls. We came up with this dish since the girls love mac and cheese and we love barbecue. Let me tell you that whenever we make it, there is always someone wanting the last spoonful.

Samantha G., Parker, TX

Really Good Fettuccine Alfredo

Serves 4

12 ounces fettuccine

1 stick butter

1-¾ cups (1 pint) heavy cream

¼ teaspoon garlic powder

½ teaspoon coarsely ground
  black pepper

1-¼ cups grated Parmesan cheese

1 Cook fettuccine according to package directions; drain and keep warm.

2 Meanwhile, in a large skillet over medium-low heat, melt butter. Add heavy cream, garlic powder, and pepper; cook 6 to 8 minutes, or until hot and well blended, stirring constantly.

3 Stir in cheese and cook 5 to 6 minutes, or until sauce is thickened. Pour sauce over fettuccine; toss, and serve.

Did You Know?

If you go to Italy, don't expect to find Fettuccine Alfredo on the menu. Even though it was created by Chef Alfredo back in the 1920's in Italy, it really only became popular when American tourists brought the dish back to the states.

Shrimp Scampi Linguine

Serves 4

1 pound linguine

1 stick butter

1 pound large shrimp, peeled and deveined, with tails left on

10 garlic cloves, crushed

1 teaspoon salt

½ teaspoon black pepper

3 tablespoons lemon juice

1 tablespoon lemon zest, optional

1 tablespoon chopped fresh parsley

1 Cook linguine according to package directions; drain, rinse, drain again, and cover to keep warm.

2 Meanwhile, in a large skillet over medium heat, melt butter. Add shrimp, garlic, salt, and pepper, and saute 2 to 3 minutes, or until shrimp turn pink and are cooked through.

3 Reduce heat to low and add lemon juice, lemon zest, if desired, and parsley; simmer 1 to 2 minutes. Toss shrimp with linguine. Serve immediately.

Serving Suggestion:
Make sure you serve this with crusty Italian bread so you don't leave any of the flavor-packed buttery sauce behind.

My Neighbor's Lasagna

Serves 6

1 pound bulk Italian sausage

1 (15-ounce) container ricotta cheese

⅓ cup grated Parmesan cheese

1 egg

½ teaspoon Italian seasoning

3 cloves garlic, minced

½ teaspoon black pepper

2 (28-ounce) jars spaghetti sauce, divided

12 lasagna noodles, prepared according to package directions

4 cups (16 ounces) shredded mozzarella cheese

1 Preheat oven to 375 degrees F. Coat a 9- x 13-inch baking dish with cooking spray and set aside.

2 In a large skillet over medium-high heat, cook sausage until no pink remains, stirring to break up sausage as it cooks. Drain off excess liquid and set aside.

3 In a medium bowl, combine ricotta and Parmesan cheeses, the egg, Italian seasoning, garlic, and pepper.

4 Spread 1 cup spaghetti sauce over bottom of prepared baking dish. Place 3 noodles over sauce. Spoon 1/3 of cheese mixture over noodles, sprinkle with 1/3 of the sausage, and 1/3 of the mozzarella cheese. Pour 1 cup spaghetti sauce over mozzarella cheese. Place 3 more noodles over the top and press down lightly. Repeat with 2 more layers of cheese mixture, sausage, mozzarella cheese, and noodles. Spoon remaining sauce over top and cover tightly with aluminum foil.

5 Bake 1 hour, or until heated through. Remove foil and sprinkle with remaining mozzarella cheese; return to oven 5 minutes, or until cheese has melted. Remove from oven and let sit 10 to 15 minutes before cutting and serving.

Serving Suggestion:

We think this is best to be made the day before you want to serve it. Not only do all the flavors blend together, it's also easier to serve. Simply cut it while it's cold, warm it and each portion comes out just perfect.

Baked Spaghetti

Serves 4

½ pound spaghetti

1 pound ground beef

¼ cup chopped onion

2 (28-ounce) jars
   spaghetti sauce

1 teaspoon garlic powder

½ teaspoon salt

2 cups (8 ounces) shredded
   mozzarella cheese, divided

1 Preheat oven to 375 degrees F.

2 In a soup pot, cook spaghetti according to package directions; drain and set aside. In the same pot over medium-high heat, cook ground beef and onion 6 to 8 minutes, or until no pink remains, stirring to crumble the beef; drain excess liquid.

3 Stir in spaghetti sauce, garlic powder, and salt. Add spaghetti and toss until evenly coated. Place half the mixture in a 2-½-quart casserole dish, sprinkle with half the cheese, then place remaining mixture on top. Cover and bake 30 to 35 minutes, or until heated through.

4 Uncover, and top with remaining cheese. Bake uncovered 5 to 7 more minutes, or until heated through and cheese is melted.

Over the Top:
To take this over the top, you can use ground Italian sausage instead of the ground beef. Also, this is awesome served with our Old-Fashioned Garlic Bread (page 21).

Good Ol' Tuna Noodle Casserole

Serves 4

1 (12-ounce) package wide egg
noodles

2 (10-¾-ounce) cans cream
of celery soup

1-½ cups milk

1 (12-ounce) can chunk tuna,
drained and flaked

1 cup shredded Swiss cheese

2 cups frozen peas

2 tablespoons butter, melted

¼ teaspoon salt

¼ teaspoon black pepper

1 cup French-fried onions

1 Preheat oven to 350 degrees F. Coat a 9- x 13-inch baking dish with cooking spray.

2 Prepare noodles according to package directions; drain.

3 In a large bowl, combine soup and milk; mix well. Add noodles, tuna, Swiss cheese, peas, butter, salt, and pepper. Pour mixture into prepared baking dish then top evenly with French-fried onions.

4 Bake 30 to 35 minutes, or until bubbly and heated through. Serve immediately

Test Kitchen *Mr. Food* *Hints & Tips*

If you want to make this in advance, just put it together and keep it chilled until ready to use. Then top with the French-fried onions, bake it off and dinner is ready.

Grilled Reuben Supreme

Serves 6

- 1 (3- to 4-pound) corned beef, cooked according to package directions
- 12 slices rye bread
- 1 cup Russian dressing
- 1 (16-ounce) package refrigerated sauerkraut, well drained
- 12 slices Swiss cheese
- 6 tablespoons butter

1 While corned beef is still warm, slice thickly across the grain.

2 Evenly spread each slice of bread with Russian dressing. Evenly top 6 slices of bread with sauerkraut, corned beef, and 2 slices of Swiss cheese. Top with remaining bread slices. Spread butter on both sides of the sandwiches.

3 In a skillet or on a griddle over medium heat, cook in batches until golden on both sides and cheese is melted.

"I used to own a NY-style deli and we were known for our Reuben sandwiches. This is a spin off of those and just as tasty. The key is to use corned beef that is cooked until it's really, really tender and still warm."
Howard R., Mr. Food Test Kitchen Chief Food Officer

French Onion Soup Burger

Serves 4

6 tablespoons butter

2 onions, thinly sliced

1-¼ pounds ground beef

1 (1-ounce) envelope onion soup mix

1 French bread, cut into 8 slices on the diagonal, lightly toasted

8 slices Swiss cheese

1 In a large skillet over medium-high heat, melt butter and cook onions 10 to 15 minutes, or until golden and caramelized, stirring occasionally. Remove to a bowl and set aside.

2 Meanwhile, in a bowl, mix ground beef and onion soup mix. Form into 4 patties and saute in the same skillet, over medium heat, 10 to 12 minutes, or to desired doneness.

3 Place burgers on toasted French bread slices. Top with caramelized onions and 2 slices of cheese. Place on a baking sheet and broil for 1 to 2 minutes or until cheese is bubbly. Place remaining bread slices on top and serve immediately.

Chicken Bacon Ranch Stuffed Pizza

Serves 4

¼ cup all-purpose flour

2 store-bought fresh pizza dough balls

⅔ cup ranch dressing

16 ounces (4 cups) shredded mozzarella cheese, divided

½ pound diced, cooked bacon

1 pound diced, cooked chicken

2 scallions, sliced

½ cup sliced black olives, optional

2 tablespoons shredded Parmesan cheese

1 Preheat oven to 400 degrees F.

2 On a floured surface, roll 1 pizza dough ball into a 14-inch circle. Place on a round pizza pan. Spread ranch dressing on dough, leaving a ½-inch border. Sprinkle with half the mozzarella cheese. Spread the bacon, chicken, scallions, and olives, if desired, over the cheese, leaving the ½ inch border. Sprinkle remaining mozzarella cheese over toppings.

3 Roll second dough ball into a 14-inch circle. Place over top of pizza, folding and pinching edges together to seal. Spray lightly with cooking spray and sprinkle Parmesan cheese on top.

4 Bake on center rack of oven 25 to 30 minutes, or until crust is golden brown.

"I am usually very traditional with my pizza, red sauce, etc. This one just works very well together. The flavors blend nicely and it has become one of our family favorites – do yourself a favor and give it a try."

Mark T., Ellsworth, WI

Secret Ingredient Sweet Potato Bake

Serves 6

- 2 (40-ounce) cans sweet potatoes, drained and mashed
- ¾ cup maple syrup
- 5 tablespoons butter, melted, divided
- 2 eggs
- ½ cup milk
- 1 teaspoon vanilla extract
- ½ teaspoon salt
- 1 cup coarsely crushed cinnamon graham crackers

1 Preheat oven to 375 degrees F. Coat a 3-quart casserole dish with cooking spray.

2 In a large bowl, combine all ingredients except graham crackers and 1 tablespoon butter; mix well. Spoon into prepared casserole dish.

3 In a small bowl, combine graham crackers and remaining melted butter. Sprinkle evenly over potato mixture.

4 Bake 35 to 40 minutes, or until firm and golden.

Special Occasion Stuffing

Serves 6

1 stick butter

1 cup chopped onion

1 cup chopped celery

1 cup dried cranberries

2 tablespoons orange zest

2 cups chicken broth

½ cup orange juice

1 (12-ounce) bag cubed
herb-seasoned stuffing

1 Preheat oven to 350 degrees F. Spray a 3-quart casserole dish with cooking spray.

2 In a large saucepan over medium-high heat, melt butter. Add onion and celery and cook 6 to 8 minutes, or until tender. Add cranberries, orange zest, broth, orange juice, and stuffing; gently stir until well combined. Spoon into prepared casserole dish and cover.

3 Bake 25 minutes. Uncover and bake an additional 15 minutes, or until heated through.

"I was never a big stuffing lover until I tried my mother-in-law's which she made only for special occasions. It was really good, and not as mushy as the stuffing I had when I was growing up. To me, the best part is the crispy crunchy part around the edges. I always make sure I grab that before anyone else at the table does."

Julie S., Anahiem, California

Mom-Mom's Ricotta Gnocchi

Serves 6

1-½ pounds ricotta cheese

2-½ cups all-purpose flour

1 tablespoon plus ½ teaspoon salt, divided

1 stick butter

3 cloves garlic, minced

¼ teaspoon black pepper

1 tablespoon chopped fresh parsley

Grated Parmesan cheese for sprinkling

1 In a large bowl, combine ricotta cheese and flour. Mix with your hands until dough is no longer sticky. On a lightly floured surface, roll ¼ of dough into a ½-inch diameter tube-like rope. Cut into ½-inch pieces and gently twist each piece. Repeat with remaining dough.

2 Fill a large pot with water, add 1 tablespoon salt, and bring to a boil over high heat. Gently drop 12 to 15 gnocchi at a time into boiling water. Gnocchi will rise to the top in 3 to 4 minutes. Cook 1 more minute, then remove with slotted spoon to a large bowl. Repeat with remaining gnocchi, then drain.

3 Meanwhile, in a large skillet over low heat, melt butter. Add garlic, remaining salt, the pepper, parsley, and gnocchi. Cook 5 to 10 minutes or until heated through, stirring occasionally. Sprinkle with Parmesan cheese and serve.

Test Kitchen Mr. Food Hints & Tips *You can flash freeze these on rimmed baking sheets. Once frozen, place into resealable plastic bags.*

"I remember going to my Mom-Mom Rusin's house on Sunday afternoons when we were little and she was always in the kitchen cooking something! She was one of those grandmothers who always wanted to feed you, whether it was a full meal or just some coffee cake or snacks. This is one of those delicious meals. Mmmm, tasty!!"

Kelly R., Mr. Food Test Kitchen
Photographer/Food Stylist

Sweet Noodle Pudding

Serves 12

1 (12-ounce) package wide egg noodles

1 (8-ounce) package cream cheese, softened

1 cup plus 1 tablespoon granulated sugar, divided

1 (16-ounce) container sour cream

1 (16-ounce) container cottage cheese

2 sticks butter, melted

6 eggs, lightly beaten

1 teaspoon cinnamon

½ teaspoon salt

2 cups cornflakes, coarsely crushed

1 tablespoon light brown sugar

1 Preheat oven to 350 degrees F. Coat a 9- x 13-inch baking dish with cooking spray. Prepare noodles according to package directions; drain and set aside.

2 In a large bowl, beat cream cheese and 1 cup granulated sugar until fluffy. Add sour cream, cottage cheese, butter, eggs, cinnamon, and salt; beat until well mixed. Stir in the noodles and pour into prepared baking dish.

3 In a medium bowl, combine cornflakes, brown sugar, and remaining granulated sugar. Sprinkle evenly over top of noodle mixture.

4 Bake 60 to 65 minutes, or until set in center.

Serving Suggestion:

No, this isn't a pudding like you might be thinking. It's more of a sweet noodle casserole that can be a served at brunch or dinner. Cut it into squares and it's good piping hot or at room temperature.

Macaroni & Two Cheeses

Serves 6

2 cups (8 ounces) shredded sharp Cheddar cheese, divided

2 cups (8 ounces) Havarti cheese, shredded, divided

1 pound mini penne pasta

4 tablespoons (½ stick) butter

2 tablespoons all-purpose flour

1 teaspoon salt

½ teaspoon black pepper

2 cups milk

16 round butter-flavored crackers, crushed (about ¾ cup)

1 Preheat oven to 375 degrees F. Coat a 9- x 13-inch baking dish with cooking spray. In a bowl, mix both cheeses together; set aside.

2 Cook pasta according to package directions; drain.

3 In a soup pot over medium heat, melt butter. Add flour, salt, and pepper; stir to mix well. Gradually add milk; bring to a boil, and cook until thickened, stirring constantly. Stir in ¾ of cheese and the pasta; mix well. Pour into prepared baking dish, then top with remaining cheese. Sprinkle with crushed crackers.

4 Bake 35 to 40 minutes, or until heated through and top is golden. Serve immediately.

Rice 'n' Pasta

Serves 5

- 4 tablespoons (½ stick) butter, divided
- 1 cup chopped onion (about 1 medium onion)
- 1 cup (about 4 ounces) spaghetti, broken into 3-inch pieces
- 1-½ cups long-grain or whole-grain rice, uncooked
- 3-½ cups chicken broth
- ½ teaspoon salt
- ⅛ teaspoon black pepper

1. In a large skillet over medium-high heat, heat 3 tablespoons butter; add onion and sauté until lightly browned. Remove from pan and set aside.

2. Heat remaining butter in skillet and brown spaghetti over medium-low heat. (Be careful -- it browns quickly.) Remove pan from heat and return onions to pan. Add remaining ingredients, mixing well.

3. Return skillet to heat, bring mixture to a boil. Reduce heat to low, cover, and cook 20 more minutes, or until all liquid is absorbed.

"This recipe has been in my family for over 30 years. We make it all the time since it is super quick and everyone loves it. (Loves it to the point that they keep going back for seconds.) So when we started collecting recipes for this book, I knew it needed to be included."
Howard R., Mr. Food Test Kitchen Chief Food Officer

Anniversary Mushroom Risotto

Serves 4

3 cups chicken broth

3 tablespoons butter, divided

1-½ cups sliced mushrooms

½ cup finely chopped onion

1 cup uncooked Arborio rice

1 teaspoon minced garlic

⅓ cup white wine

¼ cup grated Parmesan cheese

1 tablespoon chopped fresh parsley

¼ teaspoon freshly ground black pepper

1 In a saucepan, bring chicken broth to a simmer, but do not boil. Keep warm over low heat.

2 Meanwhile, in a large saucepan over medium-high heat, melt 2 tablespoons butter. Add mushrooms and onion and sauté 4 to 5 minutes, or until softened. Stir in rice, garlic, and wine; cook until wine is absorbed. Add 1 cup hot broth, stirring constantly until liquid is nearly absorbed. Repeat process, adding remaining broth 1 cup at a time, stirring constantly until each portion of broth is absorbed before adding next portion (about 15 minutes, total).

3 Remove from heat. Stir in remaining butter, cheese, parsley, and pepper. Serve immediately.

Test Kitchen. Mr. Food Hints & Tips *Don't be tempted to speed up the process. The rice needs the time to slowly cook to the right consistency.*

"I learned how to make this recipe during a private cooking class that my husband gave me as an anniversary gift. He loved it so much the first time I served it to him, that I make it every year on our anniversary!"

Mary L., Gary, IN

Walker Corn Soufflé

Serves 8

2 (15.25-ounce) cans whole kernel corn, drained

2 (15-ounce) cans creamed corn

4 tablespoons sugar

4 tablespoons all-purpose flour

4 tablespoons milk

4 eggs, beaten

1 Preheat oven to 350 degrees F.

2 In a 2 quart baking dish, combine all ingredients; mix well.

3 Bake 1 to 1-½ hours, or until top is golden.

"This corn soufflé has been making an appearance at our Thanksgiving table for as long as I can remember. Every year we contemplate replacing it with something different just to shake things up a bit. But in the end, we can never part with it. It's truly as important as the turkey at our table! In fact, we often make a second batch for ourselves, which stays hidden in the back of the fridge, to ensure we'll have leftovers, since the dish is always scraped clean."

Jennifer K., Mr. Food Test Kitchen Website Editor

Green Bean Bacon Bundles

Serves 6

½ cup Catalina dressing

1 tablespoon honey

1 (18-ounce) package frozen
whole green beans, thawed

9 bacon slices, cut in half

1 Preheat oven to 425 degrees F.

2 In a small bowl, mix Catalina dressing and honey; set aside.

3 Wrap 4 beans with a ½ slice of bacon. Repeat. Place bundles on a rimmed baking sheet and drizzle with Catalina mixture.

4 Bake 20 minutes, or until bacon is crispy.

"They're super simple, but at family gatherings, they always make an appearance and my brothers (and now my husband, too) all count the number of bundles to see how many each person gets. Inevitably, there is an odd number. (I think my dad makes an odd number on purpose.) The individuals who want the last piece must compete for it in a round of Rock, Paper, Scissors. (We all end up competing because everyone wants a second helping!)"

Brenna F., Mr. Food Test Kitchen Food Writer

Cabbage and Noodles

Serves 6

¼ cup vegetable oil

2 onions, coarsely chopped

½ head cabbage, cut into 1-inch chunks

8 ounces bowtie noodles, prepared according to package directions

½ teaspoon garlic powder

¾ teaspoon salt

½ teaspoon black pepper

1 In a large skillet over medium-high heat, heat oil; saute onions and cabbage about 15 minutes, or until very soft and light brown, stirring occasionally.

2 Add remaining ingredients and cook 7 to 10 minutes, or until heated through. Serve immediately.

Did You Know?

There are only a few recipes in this book that you will also find on our website. Why did we include this one? 'Cause it wouldn't be fair if we left out it out since everyone who tries it insists that they always want seconds...or thirds.

Creamy Spinach Casserole

Serves 4

- 4 ounces cream cheese, softened
- 4 tablespoons (½ stick) butter, softened
- ¼ cup sour cream
- ¼ cup finely chopped onion
- ¼ teaspoon garlic powder
- ¼ teaspoon salt
- ¼ teaspoon black pepper
- 2 (10-ounce) packages frozen chopped spinach, thawed and well drained
- 2 tablespoons grated Parmesan cheese
- 2 tablespoons real bacon pieces

1 Preheat oven to 350 degrees F. Coat a 1-½-quart casserole dish with cooking spray; set aside.

2 In a large bowl, combine cream cheese, butter, sour cream, onion, garlic powder, salt, and pepper; mix well. Add spinach; mix well. Spoon mixture into prepared dish. Sprinkle with Parmesan cheese and bacon pieces.

3 Bake 30 to 35 minutes, or until heated through and top is golden.

Broccoli and Cheese Soufflé

Serves 8

5 tablespoons butter, divided

¼ cup finely chopped onion

2 tablespoons all-purpose flour

½ cup hot water

1 (8-ounce) loaf pasteurized cheese product, cubed (like Velveeta)

3 eggs, beaten

2 (16-ounce) packages frozen chopped broccoli, thawed

½ teaspoon salt

¼ teaspoon black pepper

2 tablespoons plain bread crumbs

1 Preheat oven to 400 degrees F. Coat an 8-inch square baking dish with cooking spray.

2 In a soup pot over medium-high heat, melt 4 tablespoons butter; sauté onions 3 to 5 minutes, or until translucent. Stir in flour and water until smooth, and bring to a boil. Add cheese and stir until melted. Remove from heat, add eggs, broccoli, salt, and pepper; mix well. Spoon into prepared baking dish.

3 In a small microwaveable bowl, melt remaining butter in microwave. Stir in bread crumbs and sprinkle over broccoli mixture.

4 Bake 30 to 35, minutes or until set in center.

"One of my very first jobs was working for a caterer doing prep work. Although this recipe is not exactly the same, it's really pretty close to one that the caterer made over and over and over again. It was tasty and guests loved it."

Howard R.,
Mr. Food Test Kitchen
Chief Food Officer

Incredible Salads, Soups & Chilis

Asian Ramen Salad

Serves 8

1 (3-ounce) package ramen noodle soup mix

4 tablespoons (½ stick) butter

1 cup pecans, chopped

1 (16-ounce) package fresh broccoli florets

1 head Napa cabbage, shredded

1 cup matchstick carrots

4 scallions, sliced

1 (8-ounce) bottle sweet-and-sour dressing

1 Remove seasoning packet from ramen noodles; reserve for another use. Break noodles into pieces.

2 In a large skillet over medium-high heat, melt butter; add ramen noodles and pecans, and sauté until lightly browned. Drain on a paper towel-lined plate.

3 In a large bowl, toss together noodle mixture, broccoli, cabbage, carrots, and scallions; add ¼ cup dressing, tossing to coat. Serve with remaining dressing.

Test Kitchen Hints & Tips — Mr. Food

Here in the Test Kitchen we love turning inexpensive ingredients into recipes that taste like a million bucks. That's why we are excited to share with you a variation of a salad recipe that one of our viewers sent to us years ago that's always a hit.

Greek Pasta Toss

Serves 6

8 ounces rotelli or other twist pasta

½ cup Italian dressing

½ cup vegetable oil

1 tablespoon red wine vinegar

1 tablespoon grated Parmesan cheese

¼ teaspoon salt

½ teaspoon black pepper

1 (10-ounce) bag fresh spinach, coarsely chopped

8 ounces feta cheese, crumbled

1 cup whole pitted Kalamata olives

1 In a large pot of boiling salted water, cook the pasta to desired doneness; drain and cool immediately by rinsing in cold water, then drain again.

2 Meanwhile, in a large bowl, whisk Italian dressing, oil, vinegar, Parmesan cheese, salt, and pepper. Add the pasta, spinach, feta cheese, and olives, gently stirring until evenly coated. Serve or refrigerate until ready to serve (best when served at room temperature).

Lighten it Up:

To make this a bit heathier, use a whole wheat pasta instead of traditional and replace the regular dressing with a reduced fat version. There is so much taste here, no one will ever know.

Cauliflower & Broccoli Salad

Serves 6

4 bacon slices

2 cups fresh cauliflower florets, blanched (see Tip)

2 cups fresh broccoli florets, blanched (see Tip)

1 red onion, cut in half and thinly sliced

¾ cup lightly salted cashew halves

1 cup dried cranberries

1 cup mayonnaise

3 tablespoons apple cider vinegar

1 Cook bacon until crisp. Drain on paper towel-lined plate, then crumble.

2 In a large bowl, combine all ingredients.

3 Cover and chill at least 2 hours before serving.

Test Kitchen. Mr. Food Hints & Tips
To blanch the vegetables, place them in a pot of boiling water and simmer them for 1 minute; drain immediately. Place vegetables in a bowl of ice water to stop the cooking process. Drain well and they are ready to use.

Mediterranean Cucumber Salad

Serves 4

- 2 cucumbers, peeled and thinly sliced
- 4 scallions, thinly sliced
- ½ red bell pepper, chopped
- ¼ cup plain Greek yogurt
- 2 tablespoons white vinegar
- 2 tablespoons sugar
- 3 tablespoons chopped fresh dill
- 1-¼ teaspoons salt
- ¼ teaspoon black pepper

1 In a medium bowl, combine cucumbers, scallions, and red pepper.

2 In a small bowl, combine remaining ingredients and pour over cucumber mixture. Cover and chill at least 2 hours before tossing and serving.

"Living in rural Ohio, I have a large vegetable and herb garden. Every year I end up with more produce than I know what to do with. I started making this salad a few years back and it was such a hit with my church friends I wanted to share it with all of you."

Becky R., Fremont, OH

Mr. Food's Favorite Chopped Salad

Serves 6

2 cucumbers, peeled, seeded, and diced

2 green peppers, diced

3 tomatoes, seeded and diced

¼ cup chopped onion

1 (2-¼-ounce) can sliced black olives, drained

⅓ cup olive oil

3 tablespoons lemon juice

1-½ teaspoons salt

½ teaspoon black pepper

4 teaspoons white vinegar

1. In a large bowl, combine the cucumbers, green peppers, tomatoes, onion, and olives.

2. In a small bowl, combine olive oil, lemon juice, salt, black pepper, and vinegar. Pour over vegetables and stir to coat. Refrigerate 1 hour, or until ready to serve.

About This Recipe:

If you knew Art, A.K.A. Mr. Food, you knew he loved chopped salads. This was one of his favorites according to his wife, Ethel. She said that he often made a double batch when he was home on the weekends.

Panzanella Salad

Serves 8

¼ cup plus 2 tablespoons olive oil, divided

½ teaspoon garlic powder

10 (1-inch-thick) slices Italian bread, cut into 1-inch cubes

¼ cup balsamic vinegar

¼ teaspoon salt

¼ teaspoon black pepper

1 cup cubed salami

1 cup cubed provolone cheese

6 plum tomatoes, chopped

½ cup chopped red onion

¼ cup chopped fresh basil or 1 teaspoon dried basil

2 tablespoons chopped fresh oregano or 1 teaspoon dried oregano

1 Preheat oven to 375 degrees F.

2 In a large bowl, combine ¼ cup olive oil and garlic powder. Add bread cubes and toss until evenly coated. Place on baking sheet.

3 Bake 15 to 20 minutes, or until crispy and golden brown.

4 In a small bowl, whisk together remaining olive oil, balsamic vinegar, salt, and pepper until well blended.

5 In a large bowl, combine bread cubes and remaining ingredients. Add dressing; toss gently. Let stand 20 minutes before serving.

Did You Know?
Panzanella is a traditional bread and tomato salad from the Tuscan region of Italy. We've taken it to a whole new level by adding meat and cheese so you can serve it as a main dish.

Cauliflower & Broccoli Salad

Serves 6

- 4 bacon slices

- 2 cups fresh cauliflower florets, blanched (see Tip)

- 2 cups fresh broccoli florets, blanched (see Tip)

- 1 red onion, cut in half and thinly sliced

- ¾ cup lightly salted cashew halves

- 1 cup dried cranberries

- 1 cup mayonnaise

- 3 tablespoons apple cider vinegar

1 Cook bacon until crisp. Drain on paper towel-lined plate, then crumble.

2 In a large bowl, combine all ingredients.

3 Cover and chill at least 2 hours before serving.

Test Kitchen • Mr. Food • Hints & Tips

To blanch the vegetables, place them in a pot of boiling water and simmer them for 1 minute; drain immediately. Place vegetables in a bowl of ice water to stop the cooking process. Drain well and they are ready to use.

Mediterranean Cucumber Salad

Serves 4

2 cucumbers, peeled and thinly sliced

4 scallions, thinly sliced

½ red bell pepper, chopped

¼ cup plain Greek yogurt

2 tablespoons white vinegar

2 tablespoons sugar

3 tablespoons chopped fresh dill

1-¼ teaspoons salt

¼ teaspoon black pepper

1 In a medium bowl, combine cucumbers, scallions, and red pepper.

2 In a small bowl, combine remaining ingredients and pour over cucumber mixture. Cover and chill at least 2 hours before tossing and serving.

"Living in rural Ohio, I have a large vegetable and herb garden. Every year I end up with more produce than I know what to do with. I started making this salad a few years back and it was such a hit with my church friends I wanted to share it with all of you."

Becky R., Fremont, OH

Really Good Caesar Salad

Serves 4

1 cup mayonnaise

½ cup milk

2 tablespoons fresh lemon juice

½ cup plus 1 tablespoon shredded Parmesan cheese, divided

2 garlic cloves, minced

½ teaspoon salt

½ teaspoon black pepper

1 head romaine lettuce, cut into bite-sized pieces

2 cups croutons

1 (2-ounce) can anchovies in oil, drained (optional)

1 In a medium bowl, combine mayonnaise, milk, lemon juice, ½ cup Parmesan cheese, the garlic, salt, and pepper. Whisk until smooth and creamy; set aside.

2 In a large bowl, combine romaine and croutons. Add some of the dressing; toss to coat well. If need be, add more dressing or refrigerate for a later use.

3 Sprinkle with remaining Parmesan cheese and top with anchovies, if desired. Serve immediately.

Did You Know?

Although the Caesar Salad may sound like it was created in Rome it was actual the brainchild of Caesar Cardini a prominent restaurateur in Mexico. It began to grow in popularity in 1924 when his daughter, Rosa, started making it in the states. The rest is history.

Short Ribs and Cabbage Soup

Serves 12

- 2 tablespoons vegetable oil
- 2 pounds beef short ribs
- 1 head cabbage, coarsely chopped
- 8 cups beef broth
- 2 (28-ounce) cans crushed tomatoes
- 1 (6-ounce) can tomato paste
- ⅓ cup lemon juice
- 1 cup granulated sugar
- ½ cup packed brown sugar
- ½ teaspoon salt

1 In a soup pot over high heat, heat oil; brown short ribs on all sides.

2 Add remaining ingredients, bring to a boil, then reduce heat to low and simmer 2 to 2-¼ hours, or until the soup is thickened and short ribs are tender.

"My grandmother, Rose, made the best cabbage soup in the world and her trick was to add lots of short ribs to hearty-it-up. When it came to eating it, we always made sure we had not only a spoon, but a knife and fork. And you can bet that my uncles always topped each forkful of beef with a dollop of really strong horseradish. It was so good that we always needed just one more bite."

Howard R., Mr. Food Test Kitchen Chief Food Officer

Cheesy Chicken Corn Soup

Serves 6

3 (10-¾-ounce) cans cream of chicken soup

1-¾ cups chicken broth

1 (16-ounce) package frozen whole kernel corn

2 cups chopped cooked rotisserie chicken

1 (10-ounce) can diced tomatoes and green chilies

1 (8-½-ounce) can cream-style corn

1 (8-ounce) loaf pasteurized cheese product, cubed (like Velveeta)

1 garlic clove, minced

¼ teaspoon black pepper

1 In a Dutch oven, stir together soup and broth until blended.

2 Add remaining ingredients and bring to a boil over medium heat.

3 Reduce heat and simmer 20 minutes, or until smooth and thoroughly heated, stirring often.

About This Recipe:

The votes are in. This hearty one-pot soup was one of our most popular soup recipes ever. We have gotten comments from moms who swear this is the only soup their kids will eat and from many who say this is a weekly staple in their homes. With comments like that, we knew we had to include it.

Copycat Tomato Soup

Serves 6

½ of a 1 pound loaf Asiago cheese bread

3 tablespoons butter, softened

5 tablespoons butter

½ cup chopped onion

5 tablespoons all-purpose flour

4 cups milk

1-½ teaspoons salt

½ teaspoon black pepper

1-½ teaspoons sugar

¼ teaspoon oregano, plus extra for sprinkling

2 (28-ounce) cans crushed tomatoes

1 Preheat oven to 425 degrees F.

2 Make croutons for the top of the soup by slicing the bread into ¾-inch-thick slices. Butter both sides with softened butter, then cut slices into bite-sized cubes. Place cubes on a rimmed baking sheet and bake 10 to 15 minutes, or until crispy. Set aside.

3 In a large soup pot over medium heat, melt 5 tablespoons butter. Add onion and cook until softened but not browned, stirring occasionally.

4 Sprinkle flour over onion and continue to stir and cook 1 to 2 minutes. Slowly add the milk, salt, pepper, sugar, and oregano. Continue to cook and stir 8 to 10 minutes, or until slightly thickened. Add tomatoes and simmer 15 minutes, or until hot and creamy. Serve immediately topped with croutons and sprinkled with oregano.

About This Recipe:
This certainly is not your out-of-the-can everyday soup. This soup was inspired by the trendy bakery-type restaurants that are known for their soups and sandwiches. We think the oversized croutons are the best part.

Cheeseboard Onion Soup

Serves 6

3 tablespoons butter

3 large onions, thinly sliced

6 cups beef broth

¼ teaspoon salt

½ teaspoon black pepper

½ cup grated Parmesan cheese

⅓ cup dry red wine

6 (1-inch) slices French bread, toasted

1 pear, cut into wedges and sliced very thinly

6 slices mozzarella cheese

6 slices Swiss cheese

1 In a soup pot over medium heat, melt butter. Add onions and cook 20 to 25 minutes, or until golden, stirring occasionally.

2 Add beef broth, salt, and black pepper; bring to a boil. Reduce heat to low, stir in Parmesan cheese and wine, and cook 3 to 5 minutes, or until cheese is melted and soup is heated through.

3 Preheat broiler. Top each slice of bread with pear slices, a slice of mozzarella cheese, and a slice of Swiss cheese. (Stack the cheese slices crisscross.)

4 Place broiler safe soup crocks on a baking sheet. Pour soup into crocks and top each with a slice of pear-and-cheese-topped bread. Broil 3 to 5 minutes, or until cheese is melted. Serve immediately.

Test Kitchen. Mr. Food **Hints & Tips**

If you don't have crocks to serve this out of, you can melt the cheese over the bread and pear slices on a cookie sheet in the broiler for a minute or so and place them on top of each bowl of soup.

My Tailgating Chili

Serves 8

1 pound ground beef chuck

1 pound bulk Italian sausage

2 (15-ounce) cans chili beans, drained

2 (28-ounce) cans diced tomatoes, undrained

1 yellow onion, chopped

1 green bell pepper, chopped

½ cup beer

3 tablespoons chili powder

1 tablespoon minced garlic

2 teaspoons ground cumin

2 teaspoons hot pepper sauce

1 teaspoon black pepper

1 In a large soup pot over medium-high heat, cook ground beef and sausage 8 to 10 minutes, or until browned, breaking apart with a spoon. Drain off excess liquid.

2 Add remaining ingredients. Stir to combine, then cover and simmer over low heat at least 1 hour, stirring occasionally.

"Being a big Buffalo Bills fan, I live for football season and for tailgating. This recipe is one I make for every game. The rule is, the colder it gets outside, the more hot pepper sauce I add. It doesn't guarantee a win, but it does guarantee that we have a crowd at the back of my SUV before every home game."

Alan M., Amherst, NY

Backwoods Black Bean Chili

Serves 10

1 tablespoon olive oil

2 pounds boneless, skinless chicken breast halves, cut into 1-inch cubes

¼ teaspoon salt

¼ teaspoon black pepper

1 onion, chopped

1 garlic clove, minced

4 cups chicken broth

1 (14-½-ounce) can diced tomatoes

3 (16-ounce) cans black beans, undrained

1-½ cups frozen corn

1 (4-ounce) can chopped green chilies, undrained

2 teaspoons chili powder

2 teaspoons ground cumin

1 In a soup pot over medium heat, heat oil. Sprinkle chicken with salt and pepper. Add to pot with onion and garlic, and sauté 5 to 6 minutes, or until chicken is browned.

2 Add remaining ingredients and bring to a boil.

3 Reduce heat to low and simmer 50 to 60 minutes, or until chili thickens slightly, stirring occasional.

Over the Top:

Everyone in our Test Kitchen and office fell in love with this chili when they tasted it! One person tried it topped with pepper jack cheese and another with sour cream and both were a hit. Tell us on facebook which you prefer.

Delectable Desserts

Sky High German Chocolate Cake

Serves 12

- 1 (18.25-ounce) package chocolate cake mix, batter prepared according to package directions
- 2 (14-ounce) cans sweetened condensed milk
- 6 tablespoons (¾ stick) butter
- 2 teaspoons vanilla extract
- 3 cups chopped pecans
- 4 cups shredded coconut

  Pecan halves for garnish

1 Bake cake according to package directions for 2 (8-inch) round cake pans. Let cool. Cut each cake in half horizontally to make 4 layers.

2 In a medium saucepan over medium heat, combine sweetened condensed milk, butter, and vanilla. Cook about 5 minutes, or until thickened, stirring occasionally. Stir in pecans and coconut.

3 Place one cake layer on a serving platter. Spread ¼ of the coconut mixture on top. Repeat with remaining layers and garnish with pecan halves. Refrigerate until ready to serve.

Did You Know?
What we are about to share with you is surprising. German chocolate cake is NOT from Germany. It was created by Sam German, a chocolate maker from California back in 1852, and as they say…"the rest is history".

Cold Fudge Cake

Serves 12

1-½ sticks butter, melted

1-½ cups all-purpose flour

1 cup chopped walnuts, divided

2 (4-serving-size) packages instant chocolate pudding mix

3 cups milk

12 ounces cream cheese, softened

1 cup confectioners' sugar

1 (16-ounce) container frozen whipped topping, thawed, divided

1 Preheat oven to 350 degrees F.

2 In a medium bowl, combine melted butter, flour, and ¾ cup nuts. Press mixture into a 9- x 13-inch baking dish.

3 Bake 10 to 12 minutes, or until crust is firm; let cool.

4 In a medium bowl, whisk together pudding mix and milk until thickened; set aside. In another medium bowl, combine cream cheese, confectioners' sugar, and half the whipped topping; mix well.

5 Using a wet table knife, spread cream cheese mixture over top of cooled crust. Spoon chocolate pudding mixture over top of cream cheese mixture then top with remaining whipped topping. Sprinkle with remaining walnuts. Cover and chill overnight, or at least 6 hours. Refrigerate any leftovers.

"Growing up, my neighbor always made this dessert for birthdays, holidays, and block parties. So after I was married, I started making it for all occasions, and it became everybody's favorite, especially my mother-in-law's."

Patty R., Mr. Food Test Kitchen
Kitchen Director

Aunt Helen's Rum Cake

Serves 12

1 cup chopped pecans

1 (18.25-ounce) package yellow cake mix

1 (4-serving-size) package vanilla instant pudding mix

4 eggs

½ cup water

½ cup vegetable oil

½ cup rum

GLAZE

1 stick butter

1 cup sugar

¼ cup rum

¼ cup water

1 Preheat oven to 325 degrees F. Coat a 10-inch Bundt pan with cooking spray.

2 Sprinkle pecans evenly on bottom of Bundt pan.

3 In a large bowl with an electric mixer on medium speed, combine cake mix, pudding mix, eggs, water, oil, and rum; beat until blended. Pour into prepared pan.

4 Bake 55 to 60 minutes, or until a toothpick inserted in center comes out clean. Poke holes in the bottom of cake while still in pan; set aside.

5 Meanwhile, in a saucepan, combine all glaze ingredients; bring to a boil. Reduce heat to low and simmer 5 minutes. Watch carefully that it does not boil over.

6 Pour glaze evenly over hot cake in pan. Let stand one hour, or until cool. Invert cake onto platter and serve.

"This is my Aunt Helen's famous rum cake. It's served at every one of our family get-togethers since there's always a request for it. She's even been known to ship it cross-country for special occasions. No one who has ever tasted it can resist going back for one more bite, no matter how full they are."

Jaime G., Mr. Food Test Kitchen Customer Relations

Brown Sugar Banana Cake

Serves 12

¾ cup vegetable shortening

2 cups granulated sugar

3 eggs

6 bananas, mashed (about 2 cups)

2-¼ cups all-purpose flour

6 tablespoons buttermilk

1-¼ teaspoons baking soda

1 stick butter

1 cup light brown sugar

¼ cup milk

1 teaspoon vanilla extract

2 cups confectioners' sugar

1. Preheat oven to 350 degrees F. Coat 2 (9-inch) round cake pans with cooking spray.

2. In a large bowl, beat shortening and sugar until thoroughly blended. Add eggs and beat until fluffy. Fold in bananas, then fold in flour, buttermilk, and baking soda. Pour the batter equally into prepared pans.

3. Bake 35 to 40 minutes, or until a toothpick inserted in the center of each comes out clean. Allow to cool slightly, then remove to a wire rack to cool completely.

4. To make the brown sugar frosting, in a saucepan over low heat, melt the butter. Stir in brown sugar and bring to a boil for 2 minutes over medium heat, stirring constantly. Add milk; bring to a boil, stirring constantly. Remove from heat, stir in vanilla, and cool in refrigerator until lukewarm. Gradually add confectioners' sugar and beat with mixer until thick. Frost cake and serve.

Chocolate-Drenched Pound Cake

Serves 12

1 pound butter, softened

3 cups sugar

6 eggs

4 cups all-purpose flour

¾ cup milk

2 teaspoons vanilla extract

½ cup semi-sweet chocolate chips

½ cup heavy cream

1 Preheat oven to 300 degrees F. Coat a 10-inch Bundt pan with cooking spray and dust with flour.

2 In a large bowl, cream the butter; gradually add sugar, beating with an electric mixer on medium speed until light and fluffy. Add eggs one at a time, beating after each addition. Gradually add flour alternately with milk, beginning and ending with flour and mixing well after each addition. Mix in vanilla extract. Pour batter into prepared pan.

3 Bake 1 hour and 40 minutes, or until a toothpick inserted in center comes out clean. Cool in pan 10 to 15 minutes, then remove to a wire rack to cool completely.

4 To make the ganache, place chocolate chips in a medium bowl. In a small saucepan over medium heat, bring heavy cream to a boil, stirring constantly. Pour over chocolate chips and stir until mixture is smooth. Let cool 15 to 20 minutes, or until ganache begins to thicken slightly. Drizzle over cake and refrigerate until ganache is set.

We Dare You!

This is one of those cakes that is pretty hard to pass up. The cake itself is as buttery as they get and the chocolate ganache (and there's lots of that) is oh-my-gosh amazing. So we challenge you to try eating just a sliver and not going back for seconds...go ahead, we dare ya!

Black & White Texas Sheet Cake

Serves 20

2 sticks butter

1 cup water

2 cups all-purpose flour

2 cups granulated sugar

2 eggs, beaten

½ cup sour cream

2 teaspoons salt

1 teaspoon baking powder

2 teaspoons vanilla extract

¼ teaspoon baking soda

FROSTING

1 stick butter

6 tablespoons milk

4 tablespoons cocoa powder

3-½ to 3-¾ cups confectioners' sugar

1 teaspoon vanilla extract

1 Preheat oven to 375 degrees F. Coat a 10- x 15-inch rimmed baking sheet with cooking spray.

2 In a large saucepan over medium heat, bring the 2 sticks butter and water to a boil. Remove from heat; stir in flour, granulated sugar, eggs, sour cream, salt, baking powder, vanilla, and baking soda until smooth. Pour into prepared pan.

3 Bake 20 to 25 minutes, or until a toothpick inserted in center comes out clean. Cool on a wire rack.

4 To make the frosting, in a small saucepan over low heat, melt the butter with milk and cocoa powder. Remove from heat and stir in 3-½ cups confectioners' sugar and vanilla; mix well, (adding more confectioners' sugar, if necessary, until spreadable) then frost cake.

Did You Know?

It's been said that Lady Bird Johnson is responsible for creating or naming this cake. Or maybe it's because it's so big, it's been compared to the size of Texas? Either way, it's a sweet treat and you're gonna love our combination of white cake and chocolate frosting!

Back-to-Basics Coffee Cake

Serves 12

2 cups granulated sugar

2 sticks butter, softened

4 eggs

1 teaspoon vanilla extract

2 teaspoons baking powder

1 teaspoon baking soda

½ teaspoon salt

3 cups all-purpose flour

1 cup milk

½ cup mini chocolate chips

½ cup packed light brown sugar

½ cup chopped walnuts

1 teaspoon cinnamon

1 Preheat oven to 325 degrees F. Coat a 9- x 13-inch baking dish with cooking spray.

2 In a large bowl with an electric mixer on medium speed, beat granulated sugar and butter until fluffy. Beat in eggs, vanilla, baking powder, baking soda, and salt until smooth. Add flour and milk and beat 2 to 3 minutes, or until well mixed. Pour half the batter into prepared baking dish.

3 In a small bowl, combine chocolate chips, brown sugar, nuts, and cinnamon; mix well. Sprinkle half the mixture evenly over the batter in the baking dish. Pour remaining batter over that, then sprinkle the top with remaining brown sugar mixture.

4 Bake 45 to 50 minutes, or until a wooden toothpick inserted in center comes out clean. Serve warm, or allow to cool completely before serving.

"I remember my mom making this all the time for company or just for my brother, sister and me. It was a favorite in our house."
    Steve G., Mr. Food Test Kitchen CEO

Fudgy Cherry Cola Cupcakes

Makes 24

1 (12-ounce) package milk chocolate chips

1 tablespoon vegetable shortening

½ cup chopped maraschino cherries, plus 24 whole cherries drained on a paper towel, for garnish

1 (18.25-ounce) package devil's food cake mix

½ cup regular cola soda

FROSTING

3-⅔ cups confectioners' sugar

1 stick butter

6 tablespoons regular cola soda

3 tablespoons cocoa powder

1 teaspoon vanilla extract

1 Preheat oven to 350 degrees F. Line 24 muffin cups with paper liners.

2 In a small saucepan over low heat, melt chocolate chips and shortening until smooth. Dip each whole cherry into the chocolate mixture, coating completely. Place on wax paper and set aside to harden.

3 In a large bowl, prepare cake mix according to package directions using the eggs and oil called for, but replacing the water with the ½ cup cola soda. Stir in chopped cherries and evenly spoon into prepared muffin cups.

4 Bake batter according to package directions for cupcakes; let cool. Remove from pans.

5 To make the frosting, in a medium bowl, place confectioners' sugar; set aside. In a small saucepan over medium heat, combine butter, cola, and cocoa. Bring mixture to a boil, stirring constantly. Pour cocoa mixture into confectioners' sugar and beat until smooth. Stir in vanilla. Spread frosting over cupcakes and garnish with chocolate-covered cherries.

Boston Cream Cupcakes

Makes 24

1 (18.25-ounce) package yellow cake mix, batter prepared according to package directions

1 (4-serving size) package instant vanilla pudding mix

1 cup cold milk

½ cup sugar

4 teaspoons cornstarch

1 cup water

1 (1-ounce) square unsweetened chocolate

1 teaspoon vanilla extract

1 Bake batter according to package directions for cupcakes; let cool, then remove from tins.

2 Cut top off each cupcake, setting them aside, and using a spoon, scoop out a small amount of the center of the cupcake.

3 In a large bowl, whisk pudding mix and milk until pudding is thick and smooth; spoon pudding into center of each cupcake. Replace tops of cupcakes.

4 In a saucepan over low heat, combine sugar, cornstarch, water, and unsweetened chocolate. Cook, stirring constantly until the chocolate is melted and the mixture is thickened, bubbly, and smooth. Remove from heat; stir in vanilla. Let cool slightly, then spread over top of cupcakes.

5 Refrigerate cupcakes for at least 1 hour before serving, or until filling and glaze are set.

"When I was a kid, my aunt used to make Boston Cream Pie all the time. It was sort of her go-to dessert which meant it became my family's dessert of choice. Now that I'm a mom, I carry on my aunt's tradition, only I make these cupcake-size which is easier when you have two little ones and lots of their friends over constantly."
Audrey C., Newton, MA

Éclair Cake

Serves 10

1 cup water

1 stick butter, cut into quarters

¼ teaspoon salt

1 cup all-purpose flour

4 eggs at room temperature

3 cups milk

2 (4-serving-size) packages instant chocolate pudding mix

1 (8-ounce) container frozen whipped topping, thawed

¼ cup hot fudge, warmed

1 Preheat oven to 400 degrees F. Coat a 10- x 15-inch rimmed baking sheet with cooking spray.

2 In a medium saucepan over medium-high heat, bring water, butter, and salt to a boil. Add flour all at once and stir quickly with a wooden spoon until mixture forms a ball; remove saucepan from heat. Add 1 egg to mixture and beat with wooden spoon to blend. Add remaining eggs, one at a time, beating well after each addition. Spread mixture over bottom of prepared pan.

3 Bake 20 to 25 minutes, or until edges are golden brown. Remove from oven and let cool.

4 Meanwhile, in a large bowl with an electric mixer on high speed, beat milk and pudding mix until thick. Spread evenly over baked shell, then chill 1 hour.

5 When ready to serve, spread whipped topping over chocolate pudding and drizzle with hot fudge.

Bourbon Cream Pecan Pie

Serves 8

1 cup heavy cream

2 tablespoons confectioners' sugar

1 tablespoon bourbon

1 cup light corn syrup

3 tablespoons butter

½ cup firmly-packed light brown sugar

2 tablespoons all-purpose flour

¼ teaspoon salt

3 eggs, lightly beaten

1-½ teaspoons vanilla extract

1-½ cups coarsely chopped pecans

1 (9-inch) frozen ready-to-bake deep-dish pie shell, thawed

1 Preheat oven to 350 degrees F.

2 In a large bowl, beat the cream, confectioners' sugar, and bourbon until soft peaks form. Place in refrigerator.

3 In a large saucepan over medium heat, combine corn syrup, butter, brown sugar, flour, and salt; stir until butter melts. Remove from heat and add eggs and vanilla; mix well. Stir in pecans and pour into pie shell.

4 Bake 55 to 60 minutes, or until firm. Serve warm or allow to cool before serving, topped with dollops of the bourbon cream.

Over the Top:
Here in the Test Kitchen we love pecan pie but we wanted to take it to new heights. So after some experimenting, we came up with a bourbon cream that adds a subtle southern richness to what we already feel is pie perfection. What do you think?

Peanut Butter Cream Cheese Pie

Serves 8

- 1 cup creamy peanut butter
- 1 (8-ounce) package cream cheese, softened
- 1-½ cups confectioners' sugar
- 1 teaspoon vanilla extract
- 1 (12-ounce) container frozen whipped topping, thawed, divided
- 1 cup coarsely chopped peanut butter cups, divided
- 1 (9-inch) chocolate pie crust

1 In a large bowl with an electric mixer, beat peanut butter and cream cheese until smooth. Beat in confectioners' sugar and vanilla until smooth. Fold in 3 cups whipped topping and ¾ cup peanut butter cups. Spoon mixture into crust. Top with remaining whipped topping and remaining peanut butter cups.

2 Chill 8 hours or overnight, until firm.

Test Kitchen, Mr. Food, Hints & Tips

Although we love freshly ground homemade peanut butter, we recommend that you use your favorite off-the-shelf jarred variety for this recipe since it holds up much better.

Tin Roof Pie

Serves 8

- 2 cups finely crushed cornflakes
- 1 cup coarsely crushed cornflakes
- ½ cup chunky peanut butter
- ½ cup light corn syrup
- 4 cups (1 quart) vanilla ice cream, softened
- ½ cup hot fudge, divided
- ¼ cup coarsely chopped peanuts

1 Coat a 9-inch pie plate with cooking spray.

2 In a large bowl, combine finely and coarsely crushed cornflakes, peanut butter, and corn syrup. Press into prepared pie plate.

3 In a large bowl, gently stir ice cream and ¼ cup hot fudge; spread evenly into crust. Drizzle with remaining hot fudge and sprinkle with peanuts. Cover and freeze at least 4 hours or until frozen.

Did You Know?

Where does the name "Tin Roof" come from? Originally, the Tin Roof Sundae was a version of a cherry sundae sold at Chester Platt's soda fountain in Ithaca, New York. There he combined chocolate syrup and peanuts making what he called his "Tin Roof" topping based on the sound that the peanuts made when he took them out of the cans they came in. He said, "it sounded like rain on a tin roof."

Dave's Dad's Apple Pie

Serves 8

½ cup granulated sugar, plus 1
teaspoon for sprinkling

¼ cup brown sugar

2 teaspoons ground cinnamon

⅛ teaspoon ground cloves

3 tablespoons cornstarch

Pinch of salt

5 to 6 Fuji apples, peeled, cored
and cut into ¼-inch wedges

1 (15-ounce) package refrigerated
rolled pie crusts

2 tablespoons butter, cut into
pieces

1 egg white

1 tablespoon cold water

1 Preheat oven to 400 degrees F.

2 In a large bowl, mix ½ cup granulated sugar, the brown sugar, cinnamon, cloves, cornstarch, and salt. Add apples; toss until evenly coated.

3 Place 1 pie crust in a 9-inch deep-dish pie plate, pressing crust firmly against plate. Pour apple mixture into pie crust. Place pieces of butter on top of apple mixture, then place remaining pie crust over top. Trim and pinch edges together to seal. With a knife, cut four 1-inch slits in top of crust.

4 In a small bowl, beat egg white and water together. Brush over top of crust, and sprinkle with remaining granulated sugar.

5 Bake 55 to 60 minutes, or until golden brown.

"Growing up and still today, my Dad makes the world's best apple pie (don't tell my mom but it's way better than hers). After he bakes one, while it's still warm, we often sneak forkfuls right from the pie plate, it's that good. Today my Dad is a very successful chef and it's no wonder. He has a great talent for making everything taste incredible, especially his apple pie.

Dave D., Mr. Food Test Kitchen, Kitchen Assistant

Rhubarb Cobbler

Serves 12

2 (16-ounce) packages frozen rhubarb, thawed and diced

1-¾ cups granulated sugar

1 (4-serving-size) package strawberry-flavored gelatin

1 (18.25-ounce) package yellow cake mix

1 stick butter, cut into small pieces

1-½ cups cold water

1 Preheat oven to 350 degrees F. Coat a 9- x 13-inch baking dish with cooking spray.

2 Place rhubarb in bottom of prepared baking dish. Sprinkle sugar over rhubarb then sprinkle dry gelatin over sugar. Sprinkle dry cake mix over the gelatin. Place pieces of butter on the cake mix and slowly drizzle cold water over the top.

3 Bake 1 hour or until golden brown. Turn off oven and leave in another 15 minutes.

"I grow my own rhubarb and share a lot of it, too. When it's not in season, I use frozen rhubarb and it works just fine. Everyone loves this recipe and expects it to be there when we have a family gathering. It's so easy and delicious.

Barb S., Bristol, VA

Sophia's Apple Crisp

Serves 8

FILLING

- 4 apples, peeled, cored, and cut into 1-inch chunks (you can use any type of apple)
- ¼ cup all-purpose flour
- ¼ cup honey
- ¼ cup light brown sugar
- 2 teaspoons ground cinnamon

TOPPING

- 1-¼ cups instant oats
- ¾ cup light brown sugar
- ½ cup all-purpose flour
- 1 teaspoon ground cinnamon
- ½ teaspoon nutmeg
- 6 tablespoons (¾ stick) butter

1 Preheat oven to 375 degrees F.

2 In a large bowl, mix filling ingredients until well combined. Pour into an 8-inch square baking dish.

3 In a large bowl, mix topping ingredients until well combined. Sprinkle over apple mixture.

4 Bake 35 to 45 minutes, or until golden brown and crispy.

"When my mom was in high school, the "lunch ladies" were actually four wonderful women from the neighborhood who made EVERYTHING from scratch, including dessert. My mom became addicted to Sophia's apple crisp. Sophia never actually measured anything and my mom has always lived by this rule. Here's the closest my mom's come to a recipe. She and I have been making this every holiday for over 20 years and it always comes out great. Just make it with love and it'll be delicious!"

Lexi F., Mr. Food Test Kitchen
Website Editor

To-Die-For S'mores Cheesecake

Serves 12

1 (18-ounce) package refrigerated sugar cookie dough, cut into ½-inch slices

4 (8-ounce) packages cream cheese, softened

1-¼ cups sugar

2 eggs

½ cup sour cream

¾ cup all-purpose flour

1 teaspoon vanilla extract

1 tablespoon lemon juice

4 (1.55-ounce) chocolate bars, coarsely chopped, divided

4 sheets graham crackers, coarsely chopped

1 cup mini marshmallows

1 Preheat oven to 400 degrees F. Coat bottom of a 9-inch springform pan with cooking spray. Line bottom of pan with half the cookie dough slices; with your fingers, spread dough to create a solid crust. Bake 10 minutes, or until golden. Let cool. Press remaining dough slices around sides of pan to create a side crust; set aside.

2 Increase oven temperature to 450 degrees. In a large bowl with an electric mixer, beat cream cheese with sugar until smooth. Beat in eggs, sour cream, flour, vanilla, and lemon juice until well combined. Gently fold in half the chocolate pieces and all the chopped graham crackers. Spoon batter into crust.

3 Bake 15 minutes. Reduce oven temperature to 350 degrees and bake 30 more minutes. Sprinkle remaining chocolate pieces and the marshmallows over the top and broil 2 to 3 minutes, or until marshmallows are golden brown. (Be sure to keep a close eye during this step so marshmallows don't burn!)

4 Remove cheesecake from oven; let cool 1 hour at room temperature. Remove sides of springform pan; cover and chill at least 6 hours before serving.

Ricotta Cheesecake with Berries

Serves 8

2 (8-ounce) packages cream cheese, softened

1 (16-ounce) container ricotta cheese

1 cup sour cream

1-½ cups sugar

4 eggs

2 teaspoons vanilla extract

¼ cup all-purpose flour

4 tablespoons (½ stick) butter, melted and cooled

Assorted fresh berries for garnish

1 Preheat oven to 350 degrees F. Coat a 9-inch springform pan with cooking spray.

2 In a large bowl with an electric mixer, beat cream cheese and ricotta cheese until well combined. Add in sour cream, sugar, eggs, vanilla, flour, and butter. Pour mixture into prepared pan.

3 Bake 1 hour, turn oven off, and leave in oven 1 more hour. Allow to cool completely in refrigerator.

4 When ready to serve, remove sides of springform pan and garnish with fresh berries.

Did You Know?

If you leave a cheesecake in a turned-off oven after baking, it will reduce the chances of it cracking. This allows the center to set without over-baking.

Diner-Style Brownies

Makes 20

¾ cup cocoa powder

½ teaspoon baking soda

1-¼ sticks butter, melted, divided

½ cup boiling water

2 cups granulated sugar

2 eggs

1 teaspoon vanilla extract

1-⅓ cups all-purpose flour

¼ teaspoon salt

FROSTING

6 tablespoons (¾ stick) butter, softened

1 teaspoon vanilla extract

2-⅔ cups confectioners' sugar

½ cup cocoa powder

⅓ cup milk

1 Preheat oven to 350 degrees F. Coat a 9- x 13-inch baking dish with cooking spray.

2 In a large bowl, combine cocoa and baking soda. Stir in ½ the melted butter. Add boiling water; stir until mixture thickens. Stir in sugar, eggs, vanilla, and remaining melted butter; mix until smooth. Add flour and salt; mix well. Spread batter in prepared baking dish.

3 Bake 35 to 40 minutes, or until toothpick inserted in center comes out clean. Cool completely.

4 To make the frosting, in a large bowl, beat butter and vanilla; beat in confectioners' sugar, cocoa, and milk alternately until smooth. Spread frosting over brownies and cut into squares.

Did You Know?

The cocoa bean, which is where cocoa comes from, is really a fruit. And since we know fruit is good for us, these brownies must also be. Hmm, if only it was that simple!

Hawaiian Nut Blondies

Makes 20

2 cups light brown sugar

1 stick butter, melted

2 eggs

2 teaspoons vanilla extract

1- ⅔ cups all-purpose flour

2 teaspoons baking powder

1 teaspoon salt

1 cup coarsely chopped macadamia nuts, plus 2 tablespoons for sprinkling

1 cup semi-sweet chocolate chips, plus 2 tablespoons for sprinkling

1 Preheat oven to 350 degrees F. Coat a 9- x 13-inch baking dish with cooking spray.

2 In a large bowl, whisk brown sugar and butter until mixed; whisk in eggs and vanilla. Add flour, baking powder, and salt, mixing until well combined. Stir in 1 cup nuts and 1 cup chocolate chips. Spread in prepared baking dish and sprinkle with remaining nuts and chocolate chips.

3 Bake 30 to 35 minutes, or until toothpick inserted in center comes out clean. Cool then cut into bars.

"Growing up in Hawaii was the best. I remember when I was a little girl visiting my Tutu (grandmother in Hawaiian) who worked at this little coffee shop known for having the best Kona coffee on the island. This place also served a few homemade desserts to go with their coffee and these blondies were one of my favorites since they were loaded with locally grown macadamia nuts."

Malie G., Kauai, HI

Milk & Cookie Brownies

Makes 24

1 (19.8-ounce) package brownie mix, batter prepared according to package directions

1-½ cups coarsely chopped chocolate sandwich cookies, divided

2 sticks butter, softened, divided

¼ cup all-purpose flour

1 cup milk

1 cup sugar

1 Preheat oven to 350 degrees F. Coat a 9- x 13-inch baking dish with cooking spray.

2 Stir 1 cup chopped cookies into brownie batter. Pour into prepared baking dish and bake according to package directions. Allow to cool completely.

3 In a small saucepan, melt ½ stick butter; stir in flour and cook 1 minute. Slowly whisk in milk and cook until mixture thickens; remove from heat and let cool.

4 In a medium bowl, beat remaining butter and the sugar until fluffy. Beat the milk mixture into the sugar mixture until smooth. Refrigerate 30 minutes, or until spreadable.

5 Frost brownies, then sprinkle with remaining chopped cookies. Cut and serve or refrigerate until ready to serve.

About This Recipe:

We call these our Milk & Cookie Brownies since there are cookies mixed into the brownie batter and the creamy topping is a cooked milk (which some people call "boiled milk") icing. So there you go...a brownie that has it all.

Grandma Casey's Almond Roca

Serves 12

2 sticks butter, each cut into 8 pieces

1 cup sugar

6 ounces slivered almonds

1 (12-ounce) package milk chocolate chips

¾ cup finely chopped walnuts

Please note: Before you start this recipe, make sure you will be able to stand in front of the stove uninterrupted for about 10 minutes, because you must stir continuously.

1 In a saucepan over high heat, combine butter, sugar, and almonds. Stir in one direction, constantly. After 6 to 8 minutes, the mixture will reach a toffee color. You may hear the nuts start to pop before you reach the desired color. Do not stop mixing until it's done or it will separate or burn.

2 Once it reaches the toffee color, pour onto an ungreased baking sheet and spread evenly, using the back of a wooden spoon. Work quickly, because it starts to harden fast.

3 Pour chocolate chips over toffee and spread them out; let them sit for a few minutes. The heat from the candy will melt the chocolate. Spread chocolate until smooth then top with walnuts. Refrigerate until chocolate hardens, then break into pieces.

"This recipe was shared with me by my best friend, Laura. It was handed down to her from her mother-in-law, Grandma Casey from Montana. It's a tradition in her husband's family and she knew that once her mother-in-law taught her how to make this, she was officially part of the family."
Jaime G., Mr. Food Test Kitchen
Customer Relations

Glazed Hermit Bars

Makes 35

2 sticks butter, softened

2 cups firmly packed light brown sugar

2 eggs

½ cup cold water

1 teaspoon baking soda

1 teaspoon ground nutmeg

1-¼ teaspoons ground cinnamon

3-½ cups all-purpose flour

½ cup raisins

½ cup dried cranberries

1 cup chocolate chips

1 cup confectioners' sugar

2 tablespoons milk

1 Preheat oven to 350 degrees F. Coat a 10- x 15-inch rimmed baking sheet with cooking spray.

2 In a large bowl with an electric mixer, cream together butter and brown sugar. Blend in eggs. On low speed, beat in water, then baking soda, nutmeg, and cinnamon. Gradually mix in flour, about a third at a time. Stir in raisins, cranberries, and chocolate chips. Spread batter on prepared baking sheet.

3 Bake 15 to 20 minutes, or until firm. Remove pan to a wire rack to cool. When cool, cut into 2-inch bars.

4 In a small bowl, whisk confectioners' sugar and milk until smooth. Spoon glaze on each square and let sit until glaze firms up.

Frosted Peanut Butter Nuggets

Makes 4 dozen

- 1 cup creamy peanut butter
- 2 sticks salted butter
- 2 teaspoons vanilla extract
- 1 (16-ounce) package confectioners' sugar
- ½ cup white baking morsels, melted
- 2 tablespoons milk
- ½ cup finely chopped salted peanuts

1 In a large saucepan over medium heat, melt peanut butter and butter; stir in vanilla. Add confectioners' sugar and beat vigorously until well blended. Remove from heat and let cool until it can be handled.

2 Knead mixture 5 minutes, or until it gets stiff. Form into 1-inch irregularly-shaped balls (nuggets). Place on wax paper.

3 In a small saucepan, melt white baking morsels and milk over medium-low heat, stirring to combine. Drizzle over nuggets and sprinkle with peanuts.

 *You can also drizzle with melted dark chocolate for that extra special touch!*

"The basic peanut butter fudge recipe, without the vanilla and peanuts, comes from my family recipe coffer. When I started entering culinary contests, I wanted to elevate it to competition quality, so I decorated them with white chocolate and peanuts. This fudge recipe has won 1st place twice at the Indiana State Fair, which was thrilling since this isn't a cooked fudge."
Beverly R., Morgantown, IN

Toffee Potato Stick Cookies

Makes 3 dozen

2 cups plus 2 tablespoons all-purpose flour

½ teaspoon baking soda

1-½ sticks butter, softened

½ cup granulated sugar

1 cup light brown sugar

1 egg

1 egg yolk

2 teaspoons vanilla extract

1 cup chopped toffee candy bars (like Heath or Skor)

½ cup potato sticks

1 Preheat oven to 325 degrees F.

2 In a medium bowl, mix the flour and baking soda together; set aside.

3 In a large bowl with an electric mixer, cream the butter and sugars together. Add egg, egg yolk, and vanilla and mix well. Gradually add flour mixture and stir until a dough forms. Fold in toffee pieces and potato sticks. Do not overmix the dough. Chill dough 15 to 20 minutes.

4 Drop by tablespoonfuls onto ungreased baking sheets. Bake 10 to 14 minutes, or until edges are slightly brown and centers are still soft.
Let cool slightly then remove to wire rack to cool completely.

Spiced Applesauce Cookies

Makes 3 dozen

2 cups all-purpose flour

1 teaspoon salt

1 teaspoon baking soda

1 teaspoon baking powder

¼ teaspoon ground cloves

1 teaspoon ground cinnamon

½ cup shortening

1 cup sugar, plus ¼ cup for sprinkling

1 egg

1 cup unsweetened chunky applesauce

1 Preheat oven to 350 degrees F. Coat baking sheets with cooking spray.

2 In a medium bowl, combine flour, salt, baking soda, baking powder, cloves, and cinnamon; set aside.

3 In a large bowl with an electric mixer, cream shortening and 1 cup sugar until fluffy. Beat in egg. Add dry mixture gradually, alternating with applesauce. Mix until well combined. Drop by teaspoonfuls onto prepared baking sheets and sprinkle with remaining sugar.

4 Bake 10 to 12 minutes, or until nicely browned. Remove from pan to cool.

"These are the BEST COOKIES EVER, from my Great Aunt Kass. I grew up on these, and now my son loves them, too!"

Amy M., Mr. Food Test Kitchen
Office Manager

Chocolate Chip Crispy Cookies

Makes 3-½ dozen

½ cup rolled oats

2-¼ cups all-purpose flour

1-½ teaspoons baking soda

1 teaspoon salt

2 sticks butter, softened

¾ cup packed brown sugar

¾ cup granulated sugar

1-½ teaspoons vanilla extract

2 eggs

2 cups semisweet chocolate chips

1-½ cups chocolate crispy rice cereal

1 Preheat oven to 350 degrees F. In a food processor or blender, pulse oats until fine.

2 In a large bowl, combine oats with flour, baking soda, and salt. In another large bowl, with an electric mixer, cream together butter, sugars, and vanilla. Add eggs and mix until smooth. Stir in oats mixture; mix well. Stir chocolate chips and cereal into dough; mix well.

3 Drop rounded teaspoonfuls onto ungreased baking sheets, about 2 inches apart.

4 Bake 10 to 14 minutes, or until cookies are light brown. Cool 5 minutes, then remove to a wire rack to cool completely.

Good for You!

We originally came up with this recipe after we got several requests from people who were allergic to nuts, yet they still wanted a chocolate chip cookie that had crunch to it. We tried many different options and this one worked really well.

No-Bake Banana Pudding

Serves 10

1 (14-ounce) can sweetened condensed milk

1 (4-serving-size) package instant vanilla pudding mix

1-½ cups cold water

3 cups heavy cream

2 (11-ounce) packages vanilla wafer cookies

4 to 5 bananas, sliced

1 In a medium bowl with an electric mixer on low, blend sweetened condensed milk, pudding mix, and water about 1 minute. Refrigerate 10 minutes, or until firm.

2 In a large bowl, whip heavy cream until stiff peaks form. Fold the pudding into the whipped cream.

3 Place a layer of vanilla wafer cookies along the bottom of a 2-quart serving dish. Cover each wafer with a banana slice. Evenly spread half the pudding mixture over the bananas. Continue alternating layers, ending with the pudding.

4 Crush several wafer cookies in a plastic bag with a rolling pin, and sprinkle them on top. Refrigerate at least 30 minutes before serving.

NOTE: You may not need the entire second package of wafer cookies.

"I don't remember where I got this recipe, but it's the best banana pudding I have ever had. My family begs me to make this dessert and I usually make it for holidays."

Carole S., Brooklyn, NY

Fancy Schmancy Romanoff

Serves 4

½ cup sour cream

3 tablespoons brown sugar

1 tablespoon cream sherry or 1 tablespoon vanilla extract

½ cup heavy cream

¼ cup granulated sugar

4 cups assorted fresh fruit (strawberries, blueberries, raspberries, kiwi)

1 In a bowl, mix sour cream, brown sugar, and sherry.

2 In a separate bowl, beat heavy cream until it starts to thicken. Add granulated sugar and beat until stiff peaks form.

3 Fold whipped cream into sour cream mixture and mix well.

4 Keep chilled until ready to serve. Serve over fresh fruit.

Test Kitchen, Mr. Food Hints & Tips

This sauce is good over just about anything. So have fun and dress up anything from fresh fruit to pound cake with it. We've even been known to sneak a spoonful of it from the fridge for an afternoon pick-me-up!

Brownie Waffle Sundaes

Serves 8

½ cup dark chocolate chips

2 sticks butter, cut into small pieces

1-½ cups all-purpose flour

1 teaspoon baking powder

½ teaspoon salt

4 eggs

1 cup sugar

1 teaspoon vanilla extract

¾ cup milk

1 quart vanilla ice cream

1 cup chocolate sauce

Maraschino cherries for garnish

1 In a microwaveable bowl, combine chocolate chips and butter, and microwave just until chocolate is melted and smooth, stirring every 30 seconds. Set aside to cool, stirring occasionally.

2 In a large bowl, whisk together flour, baking powder, and salt; set aside.

3 In another large bowl with an electric mixer on medium speed, beat eggs and sugar 2 minutes. Slowly add the melted chocolate, vanilla and milk. With the mixer on low speed, gradually add flour mixture and mix just until combined.

4 Preheat waffle iron and coat with cooking spray (see Tip below). Pour ¼ cup batter evenly onto the prepared waffle iron. Cook about 1-½ minutes, or until edges are crispy. Carefully remove waffle with a fork. Repeat with remaining batter, spraying with cooking spray between each waffle.

5 Top with a scoop of vanilla ice cream; drizzle with chocolate sauce, and top with a cherry. Serve immediately.

Test Kitchen Mr. Food Hints & Tips

• *When making any waffles, don't pour the batter all the way to the edges of the waffle iron since the batter will spread when you close it. You can always add more or less batter after you experiment with your first waffle.*

• *Depending on the size of your waffle iron, you may need to cut waffles in half before serving.*

Caramel Nut Bread Pudding

Serves 6

12 caramel candies

1 (14-ounce) can sweetened condensed milk

2 tablespoons butter

2 teaspoons vanilla extract

¼ teaspoon salt

2 cups water

3 eggs

1 (12-ounce) French bread, cut into 1-inch cubes

½ cup chopped walnuts

1 Preheat oven to 350 degrees F. Coat an 8-inch-square baking dish with cooking spray.

2 In a saucepan over low heat, combine caramels, sweetened condensed milk, butter, vanilla, and salt, stirring occasionally until caramels melt. Remove saucepan from heat and set aside.

3 In a large bowl, combine water and eggs; beat well. Stir in caramel mixture. Add bread cubes and walnuts, and stir until evenly coated. Let stand 5 minutes, then stir again. Pour into prepared baking dish.

4 Bake 45 to 50 minutes, or until a knife inserted in center comes out clean. Serve warm.

Index

Index

J

j

j is for **j**umping. Lucy has a skipping-rope and she's learning to skip. She can get up to ten or even more. Tom can jump from the second stair, and from one paving stone to another. Sometimes he jumps on the furniture, too, though it's not really allowed.

K

k is for **k**ites, flying high up over the windy hill.

k

L l

l is for **l**ight. There's sunlight, torchlight and twilight. There are street-lights, car-lights and the fairy-lights on the Christmas tree. And there's the light that shines in from the landing when Lucy and Tom are asleep.

M

m is for **m**oon, the most magic light of all.

m

N

n is for **n**ursery school, where Tom spends his mornings.

n

O

O is for **O**ranges and **O**range-juice,
which you can suck through a straw.
O is also for **O**ven. There are some good
smells coming out of this one, but you
have to be careful because it's VERY
HOT.

P

p is for **p**ark and **p**laying.

p

Q q

q is for **q**ueens, which is one of Lucy and Jane's favorite games. Tom is supposed to hold up their trains, but he doesn't often want to.

R

r is for **r**ooms. These are some of the rooms in Lucy and Tom's house.

r

S is for **S**treets and **S**hops, Lucy and Tom have been to the supermarket with Mom. They've bought something else beginning with **S**. Can you guess what it is?

S   S

T   t

t is for **t**oys, **t**eatime and **t**elevision.

U

u is for **u**mbrellas.

u

V v

v is for **V**oices. You can whisper in a very soft, tiny voice, like this, or you can shout in a VERY LOUD, NOISY VOICE, LIKE THIS, or you can make music with your voice by singing a tune. There are cross voices and kind voices, high voices and deep voices, happy voices and whiney voices. Which kind of voice do you like best?

W

w is for **w**inter when it's too cold to play outside.
The windows have frost on them and the water
is frozen over.

When the snow comes, all the world is white.

X  **X**

X is for **X**ylophone. Lucy's xylophone has eight notes and each one makes a different sound when you strike it. You write notes in a special way, like this:

Y

y is for **y**achts on the water and **y**achtsmen on the shore.

Z

z is for **Z**oo, of course.

z is also the end of the alphabet, and
this is the end of Lucy and Tom's **a.b.c.**

AaBbCcDdEeFfGgHhIiJjKkLlMmNnOoPpQqRrSsTtUuVvWwXxYyZz